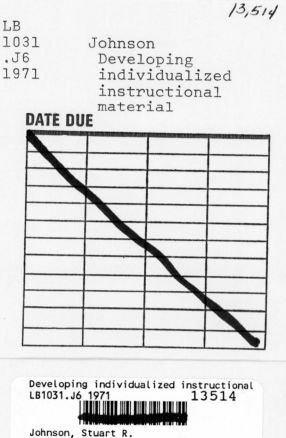

DEVELOPING INDIVIDUALIZED INSTRUCTIONAL MATERIAL

a self-instructional material in itself

Stuart R. Johnson
and
Rita B. Johnson

Westinghouse Learning Press
2680 Hanover Street
Palo Alto, California 94304

Developing Individualized Instructional Material
A Self-Instructional Material in Itself

This work is published by Westinghouse Learning Press
in cooperation with the Junior and Community College Division
of the Regional Education Laboratory for the Carolinas
and Virginia (now National Laboratory for Higher Education).

Library of Congress
Catalog Card Number: 74-146545

This publication is based on
pamphlets developed by
Rita and Stuart Johnson for RELCV.

Westinghouse Learning Press
Palo Alto, California 94304

Division of Westinghouse Learning Corporation
New York, New York 10017

Printed in the United States of America

6 7 8 9 10 11 12 77 76 75 74 73

Even the casual observer of the contemporary educational scene is aware that a new instructional technology and an empirically-based science of pedagogy are in the process of emerging. Such developments will have a drastic impact on the role of the teacher of tomorrow. At this point, a research-based approach to instruction stressing student learning (a learning-oriented system of instruction) can be developed, implemented, and fully evaluated.

The design process for instructional systems begins with the specification of instructional objectives in behavioral or measurable terms. This is followed by the diagnostic analysis of student capabilities, the optimal sequencing of course content, and the definition of relevant criterion-referenced measures of achievement. These are all combined in an empirical manner to produce a viable and efficient learning system. The system's proven capability of producing measurable learning achievement is its hallmark.

As a result of the spreading of this approach to teaching, junior college instructors become committed to accepting responsibility for student learning. "The whole system really depends on the instructor's wisdom to see and his willingness to communicate that which his students should learn and be able to do at the end of his efforts."*

However, new programs will not be developed overnight. The individual instructor remains the key to any effective program and must be convinced that students can learn. While this is not an easy assignment, it must be accomplished.

In their work with hundreds of teachers across the country, *Rita B.* and *Stuart R. Johnson* have demonstrated that, with appropriate orientation, instructors can make the crucial change to the individualized approach to instruction. This publication is the result of their efforts at developing and validating a course for teachers, designed to help them in the preparation of material necessary for the individualized instructional process.

---

*Arthur M. Cohen and Florence B. Brawer, *Focus on Learning: Preparing Teachers for the Two-Year College.* UCLA, Graduate School of Education, Occasional Reports, no. 11 (Los Angeles, 1968), p. 54.

Thanks for the early support of these efforts is owed to the UCLA Junior College Leadership Program, under the guidance of Dr. B. Lamar Johnson. The Regional Educational Laboratory for the Carolinas and Virginia and the Westinghouse Learning Press believe that this publication will be a valuable contribution to our common goal: improvement of education through teacher-assisted individualized instruction.

The Editors

CONTENTS

INTRODUCTION

Stuart R. Johnson and Rita B. Johnson

REVISION HISTORY

This self-instructional material represents the sixth version of an original series of booklets developed early in 1968 by a team interested in fostering a systems approach to instruction. The team included:

Bruce Monroe	Instructional Systems Group Seal Beach, California
Larry Harty	Instructional Systems Group Seal Beach, California
Frank Gorow	California State College at Long Beach Long Beach, California
John Nance	Fullerton Junior College Fullerton, California
Rita Johnson	California State College at Los Angeles Los Angeles, California
Stuart Johnson	Junior College Leadership Program University of California at Los Angeles

The current authors have used this material in booklet form with four groups of junior college faculty members (n=80,12,24,55). After each tryout the series was revised, based mainly on error–rate and interview data as recommended by Edling (pp. 177–194, *Rev. Ed. Res.*, Apr. '68). With regard to the last two versions, it would appear that 90% of the participants achieved at the 80% level for all chapters. Whether this achievement level results in changed classroom practice remains to be demonstrated during follow–up visits to institutions. If faculty use of these materials does not result in demonstrable student achievement, the materials will not have met their purpose and will be revised.

Rita B. Johnson
Stuart R. Johnson
Regional Education Laboratory
for the Carolinas and Virginia

PURPOSE

The overall purpose of this book is to enable teachers to improve the effectiveness of their instruction. To improve instruction, this book advocates that:

1. Course activities be broken into short segments through which learners can proceed at their own pace.

2. Achievement of learners be monitored after completion of each segment of the course.

3. Each instructional segment be revised until the desired level of achievement is attained by the learners.

An immediate aim of this book is that you, after working through these self-instructional materials, will be able to produce a short instructional package which will be tested in one of your classes and revised until it is effective. The package should be self-instructional as far as possible to permit your learners to proceed at their own pace. At the same time, it should have provisions for treatment of topics in small group or individual conferences, where the teachers can also individualize the content of the package.

Procedures listed at the end of each chapter will assist you in producing three essential components of your package: (1) objectives, (2) instructional activities, and (3) evaluation measures.

INDIVIDUALIZED INSTRUCTIONAL MATERIALS

Teachers are potentially the most sensitive, flexible, and divergently responsive components of any instructional system. Under the limitations of conventional teaching, however, they seldom have the time or opportunity to concentrate their efforts on that which teachers can do best: (1) diagnose individual learner's difficulties; (2) interact with learners when they need help on a one-to-one basis or in small group discussions; (3) inspire and motivate; and (4) identify and encourage creativity and self-direction. Self-instructional packages are essential if teachers and learners are to be free for this type of individualized instruction. However, for those who wish to capitalize on the advantages of a lecture method, these procedures are still appropriate for use in improving lecture-format instruction.

INSTRUCTIONAL OBJECTIVES

Some of you have already developed enough skill in writing objectives so that another teacher can interpret from them what the learners will be able to do by the end of instruction.

In the event that you are uncertain about how to write objectives, take time at this point to study:

Preparing Instructional Objectives
by Robert Mager (Fearon Publishers)

If this book is not available, you could use:

Educational Objectives
by W. James Popham (VIMCET Tape and Filmstrip, #1,
Box 24714, Los Angeles, CA 90024)

Remember that Mager and Popham wrote for a general audience and you may have to apply their procedures to the special problems of your own teaching area. When you have finished Mager (or Popham), resume reading the introduction.

* * * * * *

Now that you have analyzed instructional objectives, you may feel that such explicitness is suitable only for trivial, recall objectives. This impression has been called the "tragic flaw" in both Mager's and Popham's material. They selected simple objectives for the purpose of instructional simplicity. However:

> Instructional objectives can and should be made as complex and subtle as you are capable of producing! Your objectives may be primarily in the area of student intellectual growth, or your objectives may describe desired student attitudes. In any case, they must be explicit.

USE OF THE MATERIAL

A few guideline observations are in order before you begin this course:

1. Progress in working through the chapters and in producing instructional materials will be facilitated if you work with a

team, i.e., with one or more of your colleagues. You should use your team members as resource persons to critique your objectives, test items, or instructional activities and to allay (or confirm) any misgivings which arise.

2. As you work through each chapter, write in the answers to each practice exercise. This book is yours; annotate it for later reference.

3. After completing each chapter, refer to the procedure sheet at the end. It is designed to guide you step by step in the production of an individualized learning package.

PROCEDURES FOR PRODUCING AN INDIVIDUALIZED LEARNING PACKAGE

After reading each of the chapters, do the following:

1. *Chapter One*   Write a set of objectives, including one in the affective domain.

2. *Chapter Two*   Write a post–test, including measures of affect.

3. *Chapter Three*   Write an outline of a script for a sequence of instruction which provides the learner with the following: small steps, prompts, practice, and knowledge of results.

4. *Chapter Four*   Prepare materials with sufficient directions so that the learner can work through the package *without additional help from you*!

5. *Chapter Five*   Administer the package to a few learners. If objectives are not achieved, revise the package. Talking with learners will help locate inadequacies in the package.

Notes should be kept regarding development of the package and the history of its tryout, including student comments or other reasons for revision.

You are now ready to proceed to the first chapter. Good luck!

CHAPTER ONE

Specifying and Analyzing Objectives

Stuart R. Johnson

One often hears teachers say (wistfully), "I'd like my students to learn to think critically and with some originality." Although there is a degree of consensus at times on what constitutes critical thinking or originality, teachers usually admit they are uncertain about how to produce such learning. Should a teacher begin by teaching definitions and terms basic to a field and then proceed to concepts and applications? Should a teacher begin by posing a problem, then filling in terms and concepts as they are needed? Should one teach the course chronologically? Inductively? Deductively?

Any answers to these questions require attention to more fundamental questions. What are the different kinds of tasks in which the teacher wants his students to develop proficiency? What prerequisite tasks are involved and how should the learning activities be sequenced?

Thus, the purposes of this chapter are:

1. To develop your ability to apply rigorous criteria in determining the desired aims of instruction.

2. To assist you in analyzing the learning tasks which underlie a desired instructional outcome.

The exercises in this chapter have been prepared with several assumptions in mind:

1. You have accepted the importance of developing objectives as a beginning point in instructional planning.

2. Instructional objectives should be stated in terms of what the students will be able to do as the result of instruction.

3. You are applying what is learned from these pages to the development of a specific instructional plan and modifying decisions made in one stage of planning as required by decisions based upon later considerations.

You already have mastery of the essentials of the subject matter or skills which you teach. However, you may *not* have thoroughly analyzed or classified the kinds of learning tasks involved. Presumably you are interested in developing and implementing an *instructional system* for a particular group of learners with known (or assumed) beginning competencies. The comments which follow will appear more pertinent if you can refer to your own first draft of objectives for a proposed instructional plan.

The objectives of your first draft will probably need to be broken down into more specific descriptions of learner behaviors. Be sure that all the learner behaviors being sought have been included; and, given an initial set of objectives, be sure that relevant prerequisite skills are considered in your instructional plan.

Two forms of logical analysis will be used:

> *Analysis by Type of Behavior* — determining the relationship of a given objective with respect to the major categories of learning, i.e., psychomotor (skills), affective (attitudes), and cognitive (knowledge).

> *Task Analysis* — breaking a complex learning task into successively simpler subtasks, each necessary for the accomplishment of the complex task.

ANALYSIS BY TYPE OF BEHAVIOR
Three Major Types of Educational Objectives

All educational objectives can be classified as *primarily* in one of three *domains*, or large categories: psychomotor, affective, or cognitive. An example of a *psychomotor* learning objective is scoring baskets with a basketball; the objective involves controlling the muscles and making the proper motions so the ball will regularly go through the hoop. Objectives in the *affective* domain involve feelings and attitudes. An example is the learner's attitude toward a subject following the first day's introduction by the instructor. The objective is a favorable feeling toward the subject or a desire to learn more about the subject and the benefits to be gained by mastering the subject. *Cognitive* learning objectives involve intellectual processes including remembering, understanding, problem solving, and other kinds of learning which involve information storage, retrieval, and processing.

Most instruction includes some learning in all three of the domains. Often, the cognitive aspects are emphasized most, but cognitive learning also depends upon affective learning and psychomotor skills. For example, the student who has never learned to pay attention or *to attend* to a lecture (affective behavior) may have very little information to process and store (cognitive) after an hour of listening to instruction, particularly if his penmanship (psychomotor) is so erratic that he cannot review his notes.

Each of the following statements shows instructional concern about behavior classified *primarily* as psychomotor, affective, or cognitive. Label each statement with one of these three terms, P, A, or C, in the space to the left.

_____ 1. The student's interest is an important factor for success in my class.

_____ 2. In reading a micrometer, the student must get the proper "feel" as he turns the knob.

_____ 3. The important thing is to understand what you read, not just to remember what was in the chapter.

_____ 4. Tighten the nut until it is "finger tight."

_____ 5. Before you start the job, think through the steps in the procedure.

Answers: 1. Affective, 2. Psychomotor, 3. Cognitive, 4. Psychomotor, 5. Cognitive

If you had difficulty classifying the above statements, review the descriptions of the three categories of learning objectives. You might also wish to study the fuller descriptions of each classification in Appendices A, B, and C.

You have now taken the first step in the analysis of types of learner behavior — classification into one of the three major domains or categories. Various specialists also have attempted to analyze educational objectives within each of the three domains.

Psychomotor Objectives

Among those who have analyzed the performance of responses requiring muscular coordination (the psychomotor category) is Elizabeth Simpson.* Her classification is abstracted below and is presented in greater detail in Appendix A. She proposes that the five categories be arranged in increasing complexity, and that the first step is necessary to the completion of the second, and so on.

Which of the two objectives below is the more complex?

_____ 1. Student shall grasp the tennis racquet handle as if he were shaking hands with it.

_____ 2. When hitting the ball, student shall not let the racquet head drop below the handle.

ANSWER:

Holding the racquet properly is a necessary preliminary to hitting the ball with the racquet in proper position; therefore, the second objective is more complex.

Now examine the psychomotor classification which follows:

LEAST COMPLEX   *Perception* – becoming aware of a situation which may result in a muscular response

Set – adjustment or readiness for a particular kind of action

Guided response – imitation of another person performing an act or trying various responses in trial–and–error fashion

Mechanism – habitually correct response

MOST COMPLEX   *Complex overt response* – performing a complex act correctly with ease and without hesitation

---

*Elizabeth Jane Simpson, "The Classification of Educational Objectives, Psychomotor Domain" (Project report, University of Illinois, 1966).

At what level of the psychomotor classification is each of the objectives below?

_____ 1. Student shall grasp the tennis racquet handle as if he were shaking hands with it.

_____ 2. When hitting the ball, student shall not let the racquet head drop below the handle.

Objective 1 should have been labeled *Set* and Objective 2, *Guided Response* or higher, depending upon whether the student is beginning to gain this skill or is displaying the skill on a habitual basis. Objective 1 is the physical readiness necessary to hit the ball and therefore is placed in the *Set* category. Appendix A contains more complete descriptions of each category.

Affective Objectives

Among those analyzing the affective category are David R. Krathwohl and his colleagues.* Their classification is presented in Appendix B and a modified version follows below. If you and your colleagues are to design an instructional system which leads to predictable achievement by learners, you should not ignore the attitudes and feelings of the learner. It may be that something in the affective category will make the difference between failure and success on a particular cognitive objective. The affective classification is arranged to show increasing levels of personal acceptance.

LOW ACCEPTANCE *Receiving or attending* — awareness (of form, color, differing viewpoints, importance of something), willingness to receive (as shown by hearing viewpoints of others or accepting differences), and controlled or selected attention (as shown by listening with discrimination or by sensing importance of details)

Responding — acquiescence or compliance, willingness to respond, and satisfaction in response (as shown by expressing pleasure)

---

*David R. Krathwohl et al., *Taxonomy of Educational Objectives, Handbook II: Affective Domain* (New York: McKay, 1964).

Valuing – acceptance of a value, preference for a value, and commitment or conviction (as shown by being loyal or attempting to influence others)

Organizing – developing a value system (as shown by identifying the characteristics of something valued or by making plans concerning social problems)

HIGH ACCEPTANCE *Characterization* – developing an ethical code or a philosophy of life (as shown by consistent behavior)

This outline of affective terms arranges in sequence the feelings and the emotional responses which are usually labeled *interest, attitude, appreciation,* and *values.* The range is from simple attention to the development of a value system. The two lower levels, *receiving or attending* and *responding,* are basic to all successful instruction. The higher levels are concerned with personal and interpersonal adjustment, value formation, and character development.

See if you can judge which two of the following objectives are low in terms of acceptance. Then decide which two are high in acceptance. Write *L* or *H.*

_____ 1. Student reads newspaper editorial on freedom of speech when assigned as homework.

_____ 2. Student defends a fellow student's right to advocate government censorship of news.

_____ 3. Student listens to what is said during class discussion on freedom of speech.

_____ 4. During class discussion student describes the history and underlying assumptions in his advocacy of free speech.

ANSWER:

Numbers 1 and 3 are low; numbers 2 and 4 are high. If your answers do not correspond, it may be helpful to review the affective classification in Appendix B. The four objectives above are in the following categories: 1. Responding; 2. Characterization; 3. Receiving; 4. Organizing.

It is obvious that affective objectives are important to instruction. For example, it is difficult to imagine a successful instructional program which fails to capture the student's attention or fails to make him willing to respond. Furthermore, most instructors care deeply about developing a positive attitude among students toward the subject of instruction. Pure cognitive learning without expression in the real life of the student is a futile exercise.

Cognitive Objectives

A practical classification of cognitive learning objectives was developed by Bloom and his colleagues. This classification is arranged in terms of complexity. Its chief value to instruction is in helping to call the teacher's attention to more complex objectives than mere memorization and recall. The complete classification system is summarized below from the original, which is in Appendix C. You should review the original for examples and further explanation.

LEAST COMPLEX   1.0 *Knowledge* or ability to recall information (memory)

   1.1 Knowledge of specifics — facts, definitions, symbols

   1.2 Knowledge of ways of dealing with specifics — forms and conventions, steps in a process, categories, etc.

2.0 *Comprehension* or understanding

   2.1 Ability to translate or rephrase

   2.2 Interpretation or recognition of the essentials

   2.3 Extrapolation or recognition of implications and limitations

3.0 *Application* or transfer — ability to use knowledge and understanding in a novel situation to solve problems

4.0 *Analysis* or breaking a whole into its elements; analysis of relationships or organizational principles

5.0 *Synthesis* or putting together elements and parts to form a new whole

MOST COMPLEX 6.0 *Evaluation* or making judgments using internal evidence or external standards

Achieving competence at any level in the cognitive classification requires competence at successively lower levels. For example, to explain the meaning of a word by saying "in other words" (2.1) requires memory of the given definition (1.1).

Try classifying the following instructional objectives into one of the following levels: knowledge, comprehension, or application. Write *K, C,* or *A*.

———— 1. Student gives the appropriate English equivalents of forms of greetings in French, but not exact translation.

———— 2. Given the names of three contemporary composers, student shall give the name of one composition by each.

———— 3. Student can explain in his own words the meaning of a political cartoon.

———— 4. Student shall convincingly represent a member of a taxpayer's association during a mock meeting of the city council.

ANSWERS: 1. Comprehension; 2. Knowledge; 3. Comprehension; 4. Application

The conditions for learning can best be met when the nature of the learner's tasks is understood. These depend, in turn, upon the level of complexity of the objectives. If the learning task involves *memory* only, ways are needed to help the student remember, and the student should be given practice sessions in remembering. If the learning task involves comprehension of an idea or a technical term, something more than memory is involved, for memory alone will not help the learner to "explain in his own words." The student will need practice at rephrasing ideas or concepts to develop competence. Similarly, the student should be given practice at whatever cognitive level is sought.

Summary

You now have three frameworks for analyzing learner behavior. You have seen that all objectives can be classified primarily into one of three categories: psychomotor, affective, or cognitive. The psychomotor classification scheme describes muscular responses at five levels of complexity: perception, set, guided response, mechanism, and complex overt response. The affective domain has been divided into five classes: receiving or attending, responding, valuing, organizing, and characterizing behavior. The cognitive category has been subdivided into six classes: knowledge or memory, comprehension, application, analysis, synthesis, and evaluation; some of the classes have been subdivided further.

TASK ANALYSIS

You have been looking primarily at the type of behavior which the learner is to develop. Now change your perspective to examine the sequences of the learner's tasks as he practices for mastery of a behavior. These are the same objectives but they are viewed from a different viewpoint. Since analysis means "breaking down into simpler elements," the next step is to examine learning tasks to identify subtasks upon which mastery of the terminal task depends.

Task analysis is essential in a systems approach to instruction: it makes mastery of a subject possible by identifying small (component) learner steps, each of which can be mastered with adequate learner practice.

For example, a person who has never seen the pilot's compartment of an airplane can learn to fly the plane if the process is broken down into small enough steps, properly sequenced, so that each step can be mastered before the next is attempted. Faulty task analysis or improper sequencing can lead to learning failures.

> *Task analysis* means breaking down a learning task (an objective) into component tasks, each of which must be mastered as a prerequisite to mastery of the total task.

To analyze a learning task, first state the terminal objective precisely When phrased in terms of the learner behavior, the objective tells what the learner will be able to do after the instruction. To analyze the over-all task, ask questions like: What must the learner be able to do to achieve the objective? What kinds of learning are involved? What prior skills are necessary? What specific knowledge is required? What concepts or meanings must be understood? What is prerequisite to ultimate success?

In cognitive learning, the classification suggests the sequence in which learning tasks can be presented. For example, to apply a principle in a new situation, the learner must understand (be able to explain) the principle and recall acceptable words and phrases to use in speaking or writing about the principle. However, most learning tasks include a number of subtasks.

For example, suppose an objective in a college English class were stated like this:

> To be able to write a one–page expository
> paper supporting a political point of view.

What is the nature of the task? Since our frame of reference is college English, it is assumed the student already possesses the psychomotor skills of handwriting or typing; so these can be ignored in the task analysis or added as objectives. Before he can write such a paper, how-ever, the student must be able to tell the difference between a paper *about* some topic or political viewpoint and one which *supports* a political point of view. The learner who has mastered this subtask (by practicing this kind of discrimination) has a clearer view of his goal and of his assignment.

What else is required to write an expository paper? To say that a paper is made up of paragraphs, that paragraphs are made up of sentences, and that the abilities to compose each are subtasks is to over simplify the task. To illustrate, one subtask is to write the introductory para-graph — which is different from other types of paragraphs. What is re-quired to write a good introductory paragraph? If *arousing interest* is one of the requirements, what does interest arousal require? Does it involve choice of words, length of sentences, a particular type of sentence, or the arrangement of sentences in the opening paragraph? If the learner's task (or subtask) is *problem solving* (the problem being to write a paragraph which will arouse interest), what are the steps in solving the problem and what are the requirements at each step?

Below is an example of a simple task analysis, one of many that could be logically derived from the previous objective.

TASK ANALYSIS: To Write a One-Page Expository Paper

Subtask 1: To discriminate between a well-written paper and one which does *not* meet the instructor's criteria

> **Subtask a:** To remember all of the instructor's criteria, or to review the list supplied, asking successful questions about unclear criteria

> > **Subtask (1):** To find out what the criteria are, if the previous list is misplaced

Subtask 2: To write an introductory paragraph which arouses interest

> **Subtask a:** To discriminate between paragraphs which arouse interest and paragraphs which do not do so with particular readers

> **Subtask b:** To identify the elements of a paragraph which arouse interest

> **Subtask c:** To select "arousal" words and phrases

> **Subtask d:** To write an introductory sentence which attracts attention

> > **Subtask (1):** To discriminate between sentences which attract attention and those which fail to do so

> **Subtask e:** To evaluate the paragraph as written, using the criteria of a good introductory paragraph, and/or to elicit the evaluation of peers or instructional staff

Subtask 3: To write a paragraph which supports a viewpoint

> **Subtask a:** To discriminate between paragraphs which support a viewpoint and paragraphs about a viewpoint

Obviously each of the subtasks implies other subtasks.

> WHERE YOU STOP IN THE DERIVATION
> OF SUBTASKS IS A FUNCTION OF WHERE
> YOU CHOOSE TO HAVE YOUR INSTRUC-
> TIONAL RESPONSIBILITY BEGIN.

For a practice exercise in task analysis, consider a straightforward problem in training a grocery checker to calculate the individual price of group-priced items.

Objective: Within 10 seconds student can correctly calculate the cost of one grocery item, given the cost of several such items, for example, 2/67¢, 4/25¢.

List two subtasks which are prerequisite to attainment of this objective.

Task Analysis:

1. _____

2. _____

To determine the adequacy of your task analysis, it is likely that two important subtasks are:

1. Student can correctly divide two–digit numbers by the num-bers 2 through 9 and round off.

2. Student can correctly multiply two–digit numbers by one–digit numbers.

More fundamental subtasks might include:

a. Student can state that "any fraction of a cent should raise the cost of the item to the next higher whole cent."

b. Student can translate the symbol *2/67¢* into the statement *two of these items cost 67¢.*

To further validate a list of subtasks, you should consult a fellow teacher and obtain his agreement that your subtask items are prerequisite to the objective. When you are attempting this process in your own teaching, a colleague is a reasonable source to validate your task analysis.

Summary

Success in any task depends upon success in the prerequisite tasks, i.e., upon attaining the prerequisite skills, knowledge, and understanding. Therefore, prerequisites for any task must be identified. The learner must have previously acquired them or be provided practice in them at the time they are needed. The learner's success in any task depends, in part, upon the instructor's planning: upon identifying the prerequisites, upon determining whether the learner does (or does not) have them, and upon assuring that the learner has mastered them. An effective task analysis, therefore, includes subtasks which identify the kinds of learning essential for attainment of the objective.

Now take the criterion test to determine whether this material has been effective and whether the objectives of this chapter have been achieved. The minimum acceptable performance for this chapter is that 90% of the participants score 90% or better.

CRITERION TEST

Place a *P*, *A*, or *C* by each objective depending upon whether it is *primarily* psychomotor, affective, or cognitive:

_____ 1. Student shall draw an inked line with no discernible deviation in width.

_____ 2. Student can correctly select the phrase describing 10 common map symbols.

_____ 3. Student can summarize the arguments of two peers to the satisfaction of each.

_____ 4. Student will request that campus discipline regulations be revised by a student committee.

_____ 5. Student can apply bandage without impairing sterility of the pad.

_____ 6. Fewer than 10 percent of the students shall drop a class during the first 3 weeks.

Read the two psychomotor objectives and place an *X* by the objective which is more complex.

_____ 7. Student shall fill the hypodermic syringe without admitting air bubbles into the syringe.

_____ 8. Student shall slowly advance the hypodermic needle into tissue near the surface of the wound, maintaining constant pressure on the syringe plunger.

In the following three objectives, write *High* by the objective which is highest on the affective hierarchy and write *Low* by that which is lowest.

_____ 9. Student states that watching an assigned TV documentary program was interesting.

_____ 10. Student watches a film in class.

_____ 11. Student searches TV Guide for programs on science for his leisure viewing.

One example of a cognitive objective at each of the knowledge levels, comprehension, application, and analysis, is given below. Place the letters *K, C, Ap,* and *An* in the appropriate blanks.

_____ 12. In his own words, student will state the meaning of the term *social system.*

_____ 13. After observing a public picnic ground, student shall decide which social subgroups were present; he shall give them descriptive names and shall state observations to defend his classification.

_____ 14. Student will correctly define the terms *status* and *hierarchy.*

___ 15. Given (1) an elementary school class roster and (2) the name of the pupil selected by each pupil as "my best friend in class," student will identify the most popular pupils and the social isolates.

Place an X by those subtasks which are necessary to the accomplishment of the objective: Students shall swim 50 yards using breast stroke.

___ 16. Student can locate small object on bottom of pool.

___ 17. Student must tread water for 15 seconds.

___ 18. Student shall coordinate arm stroke and kick.

___ 19. Student shall coordinate breathing and arm strokes.

___ 20. Student shall shower before getting into public pool.

Check your answers with the key on page 24. Then fill out the Revision Data sheet on page 25 and mail it as instructed.

ANSWERS TO THE CRITERION TEST

1.	P	6.	A	11.	High	16.	
2.	C	7.		12.	C	17.	
3.	C	8.	X	13.	An	18.	X
4.	A	9.		14.	K	19.	X
5.	P	10	Low	15.	Ap	20.	

DEVELOPMENT PROCEDURES

You are now ready to begin the first step in the production of a self-instructional package for use by classroom learners.

1. Identify your target learners.

2. Write a set of objectives specified in behavioral terms which your package will be designed to accomplish.

3. Include in your objectives at least one in the affective domain.

4. Determine the approximate learning time needed for the learner to accomplish the objectives. Limit your set of objectives at this point to those which can be accomplished in a brief period of time (e.g., from 10 to 60 minutes).

5. Consult one to three peers and determine whether your objectives are behaviorally stated.

REVISION DATA SHEET — CHAPTER ONE

PLEASE COMPLETE THIS SHEET AND MAIL TO:

WESTINGHOUSE LEARNING PRESS
2680 HANOVER STREET
PALO ALTO, CALIFORNIA 94304

INSTRUCTIONS: As you work through these chapters you will realize that the authors are committed to the use of achievement data to revise instructional materials and procedures.

Please review your answers to the practice exercises in the chapter. Mark below any exercise where your answer did not match the "correct" answer. By doing this you will help us identify areas in the chapter where *we have failed* to provide adequate instruction. Please feel free to comment on your reasoning or sources of confusion for any exercise which you missed (i.e., we failed). Also, mark any criterion test item which you missed. Be assured that this revision data sheet will be reviewed by us with intense interest! Your response will guide our revisions.

The Johnsons

Practice Exercises:		Criterion Test:	
Page		Page	
11. _____	1.	21. _____	1.
_____	2.	_____	2.
_____	3.	_____	3.
_____	4.	_____	4.
_____	5.	22. _____	5.
12. _____	1.,2.	_____	6.
13. _____	1.	_____	7.,8.
_____	2.	_____	9.
14. _____	1.	_____	10.
_____	2.	_____	11.
_____	3.	_____	12.
_____	4.	_____	13.
16. _____	1.	_____	14.
_____	2.	23. _____	15.
_____	3.	_____	16.
_____	4.	_____	17.
20. _____	1.	_____	18.
_____	2.	_____	19.
		_____	20.

Name	Teaching Area	School	Date

CHAPTER TWO

Measuring Attainment of Objectives

Stuart R. Johnson

Obtaining Evidence of Learner's Achievement of Instructional Objectives*

Systematic approaches to the development of instructional programs invariably stress the need to define the goal or objectives in terms of student behavior. From the behaviorally stated objectives, it is possible to derive specific measuring procedures (criterion measures) to obtain evidence of program effectiveness. Regardless of the type of desired outcome of any system, information is needed regularly on whether the predicted outcome (objective) is gradually being accomplished. Obtaining this information is referred to as a measurement process. The process consists of two steps: some sort of observational comparisons and means to record the observations.

For the purpose of this chapter, three uses of measurement data are important. In an instructional setting, these three uses may be illustrated as follows:

1. Measurement data may be fed back to the learner immediately. This instructional practice is referred to as *reinforcement* for correct responses or giving *knowledge of results,* as implied when directions are given to the learner for his next step (review, restudy, or continue on to new tasks).

2. Measurement data may be used to accept or reject an instructional system. For example, a teacher might conclude, on the basis of poor learner performance, that a given workbook is unsatisfactory and should not be used again.

3. Measurement data may be used to improve an instructional procedure or system.

The last consideration is the basis for this chapter. Although the first two considerations are perfectly appropriate uses of measurement data, this chapter is mainly concerned with measurement procedures for upgrading the effectiveness of the instructional system through repeated revision.

---

*Some of the procedures are described more fully in a most helpful and entertaining paperback: Eugene J. Webb et al., *Unobtrusive Measures: Nonreactive Research in the Social Sciences* (Chicago: Rand McNally, 1966).

In the previous chapter (Specifying and Analyzing Objectives), you undertook the development of a variety of instructional objectives. Now you will develop a rationale for measurement procedures which provide evidence of the learner's achievement of these objectives. Your objectives in this chapter are:

1. You will be able to recognize a number of measurement procedures which can serve as criterion measures for the instructional objectives.

2. You will be able to distinguish product from process criterion measures as well as reactive from nonreactive measures.

3. You will be able to distinguish minimum performance standards from either instructional objectives or their criterion measures.

CRITERION MEASURES

Once a set of instructional objectives has been selected, procedures must be developed to gather evidence on whether the objectives have been met. Problems of confusion and learner misdirection arise if these evidence-gathering procedures are not made specific prior to instruction. For example, consider the following objective:

> The learner shall commit himself to a position
> with regard to Fair Housing.

There is *no* way to know (when later trying to gather evidence of student learning) whether the instructor wanted the learner to:

- sign a petition
- write a letter to a legislator
- write an essay on Fair Housing
- raise objections in class discussion about unfair housing practice
- ask for the address of a local ACLU chapter
- volunteer to head up a committee on Fair Housing practices
- simply state in a paper-and-pencil test that he favors Fair Housing legislation.

Any of these behaviors might reflect commitment. For this reason, it is important that the instructor make explicit in his plans (in advance of instruction) the criterion measures he will use to determine whether the objective has been achieved.

> CRITERION MEASURES ALLOW THE COL-
> LECTION OF EVIDENCE OF CHANGE IN
> BEHAVIOR, THUS GIVING EVIDENCE OF
> INSTRUCTIONAL EFFECTIVENESS.

Examples of criterion measures include any procedure which *yields a numerical index of performance.*

1. Multiple-choice or true-false test with scoring key

2. Rating scale or scoring sheet for essay questions, constructed response, term papers, book reports, etc.

3. Check sheet, rating scale, interview schedule, or observational record form to measure a student's verbal or psychomotor performance

4. Counts or tallies of types of observed behavior

To clarify the relationship between objectives and criterion measures, examine the following objective and criterion measures and mark the alternative which describes a criterion measure for the objective.

Objective: The learner will recognize examples of inductive reasoning.

Alternative A: Learner underlines those sentences in a newspaper editorial which constitute inductive argument.

Alternative B: Learner reads the textbook description of deductive vs. inductive reasoning.

Alternative C: Learner writes short essay in which he describes the essential characteristics of inductive reasoning.

Alternative A describes a situation in which the learner *recognizes examples of inductive reasoning,* the behavior called for in the objective.

By contrast, Alternative B describes an activity which assists the learner in *achieving* the objective, but it does *not* result in an index of the learner's ability to *perform* the behavior described in the objective. Alternative C gives evidence of the learner's descriptive capabilities but does *not* tell whether the learner can *recognize* examples of inductive reasoning. Only Alternative A describes a criterion measure which yields a numerical index of performance.

If you are still uncertain about criterion measures, try this example. Which alternative describes a criterion measure for the objective shown?

Objective: Learner will calculate prices of items of merchandise which are to be discount priced during a "1/3 off" sale.

Alternative A: Learner explains the procedure by which percentages are calculated.

Alternative B: Learner prepares price tags for sale items originally priced at $1.98 and other common prices.

Alternative C: Learner assists parent in choosing a lower-priced product from alternatives on sale in the supermarket.

The correct answer is Alternative B since the objective indicates that the student will *calculate* rather than simply describe a procedure for making the calculations. The criterion measure is the number of correctly completed sales price tags, i.e., the numerical index of performance is the number of accurate pricings out of the total possible (in the form of correctly filled-out price tags).

Instructors often focus exclusively upon the use of paper–and–pencil tests as criterion measures without taking advantage of other types of evidence–gathering procedures. To assure that a broad variety of criterion measures has been considered, two schemes are suggested.

1. Product vs. process criterion measures

2. Reactive vs. nonreactive criterion measures

PRODUCT-PROCESS CRITERION MEASURES

The product-process distinction is quite straightforward. A teacher might express the distinction by saying: "I can assess a student's performance by watching him in action or by examining what he makes." This idea underlines the distinction between product and process measures.

- *Product measures* give tangible evidence of a learner's performance which can be stored or filed for later reexamination if desired.

- *Process measures* involve the collection of evidence of a learner's performance only as it occurs.

Which of the following is a product measure?

　1. Procedure which measures what learners have constructed

　2. Procedure which measures what learners are doing

The first statement describes a product measure; the second describes a process measure.

The examples below help clarify the product-process distinction.

Product Measures	*Process Measures*
Procedures for comparing:	Procedures for comparing:
1. any written responses such as those on tests, term papers, essays, book reports	1. any spoken responses such as those made in dramatizations, public speaking, foreign language, technical discussion
2. any constructed materials such as paintings, musical scores, diagrams, maps, devices, models	2. any psychomotor performance such as the form used while stroking keys of a musical instrument, throwing a baseball, pouring liquid chemicals

Of the learner's performances below, indicate which involve "product" criterion measures and which involve "process" criterion measures. Write *Prod* or *Proc*.

The learner will:

_____ 1. prepare a circuit diagram

_____ 2. write a short poem about childhood

_____ 3. question a fellow student without arousing hostility

_____ 4. open a student government meeting with the Pledge of Allegiance

One and two yield tangible products which will require procedures for rating the product. Three and four require establishing procedures for observing and rating learner performance as it occurs.

In the list of criterion measures below, indicate in the same fashion whether each is a product or a process measure.

Rating scales or scoring sheets for:

_____ 1. interpretive reading of a eulogy

_____ 2. a contour map drawn from given elevations

_____ 3. a half-gainer dive

_____ 4. a flow diagram

_____ 5. signalling a right-hand turn

You were correct if you indicated the following answers:

    1. Proc

    2. Prod

    3. Proc

    4. Prod

    5. Proc

REACTIVE AND NONREACTIVE CRITERION MEASURES

Now look at the second scheme, mentioned earlier, which can help generate a broader variety of criterion measures.

> THE TERMS *REACTIVE* AND *NONREAC-TIVE* SUGGEST THAT SOME MEASURES MAY BE REACTIVE, i.e., MAY CHANGE THE NATURAL RESPONSE NEEDED IN PROMPTING AND MEASURING.

For example, students often speak of the desirability of "psyching out" the instructor to know what position to take during class discussions or in answering test questions. Therefore, common standard testing procedures such as quizzes and examinations represent examples of reactive measures, at least to the extent that the students know the kinds of responses previous instructors have looked for.

To illustrate, suppose that an instructor in a health science class asks his students to list reasons for (or against) the practice of smoking marijuana. If the students are aware that the instructor's scoring procedures will reward only those reasons given for not smoking marijuana, then this measurement via a test question represents a *reactive* criterion measure since it leads the students to modify the responses they might otherwise have given.

Examples of less reactive measures in this context might be:

1. submitting a *"contemporary word meanings"* questionnaire where students are asked to match words common to the marijuana smoking subculture with their meanings in everyday English

2. observing and recording how students choose sides in a proposed debate on the topic *"Should Marijuana Be Legalized?"*

Suppose a speech instructor is concerned that students use particular speech practices which he is trying to strengthen. Which of the following criterion measures is likely to be less reactive and result in the more accurate data?

_____ 1. Listening to a 60-second impromptu talk in class

_____ 2. Listening to a classroom discussion of a controversial topic, among peers, in a "buzz session"

It is more probable that the discussion with peers will be less reactive and that speech habits will emerge more naturally in the "buzz session" than in the speech to the class.

In each of the situations below, select the criterion measures which you feel would be less reactive.

1. Instructor decides to determine the extent to which his class is doing outside reading of reference materials.

_____ He tallies the number of hands raised in response to the question "How many were able to do some reference reading?"

_____ He tallies the number of enrollees' names on a library checkout sheet for reference materials.

2. A typing instructor hopes that students will use the correct form for letters of correspondence.

_____ He assigns students to submit a letter (to a hypothetical company) requesting an appointment for an employment interview; letters are obtained and scored.

_____ He asks that students write and mail a "thank you" letter to a guest speaker who visited the class; letters are obtained and scored.

You are correct if you selected the second option in both cases. Both of the first alternatives are more likely to make the students aware of the desired behavior sought by the instructor.

SETTING STANDARDS OF MINIMUM ACCEPTABLE PERFORMANCE

So far, you have been urged to consider a variety of criterion measures which enable you to assign a performance index (e.g., a score) or performance indices (e.g., multiple scores) to observations of student behavior. Thus, when you obtained a series of scores or performance indices after instruction, you were then (and only then) in a position to decide whether the instructional program measured up to expectation or needed revision. Making the decision on what you set as a standard of acceptable performance by the learner is called *setting minimum performance standards.*

For example, suppose that an instructor has decided that he wants learners:

1. To identify common insects by their scientific names.

He obtains 10 pictures of common insects and tells his students:

2. Look at each picture carefully and then write in the blank on your answer sheet the scientific name of each insect. You will be given one point for each name that is correct according to the identifications given in your textbook.

Then he decides that the instructional program shall be deemed successful if:

3. 80% of the students correctly write the scientific names of 90% of the insects pictured.

Now, reread the three statements and decide which is the instructor's overall *objective*, which is the statement of the *criterion measure*, and which statement describes *minimum performance standard.*

1. _____

2. _____

3. _____

You probably recognize that the last phrase represents the *minimum performance standard*, and the first phrase represents his general *objective*. Obviously, the middle phrase describes the *criterion measure.*

MULTIPLE CRITERION MEASURES

In attempting to obtain evidence of the learner's ability to perform the behavior described in the instructional objective, it is desirable to employ several different kinds of criterion measures. The use of multiple criterion measures produces a more reliable estimate of performance than any single measure. Multiple criterion measures are called for especially in those cases where a measure is (1) difficult to obtain, (2) predictably reactive, or (3) obtainable only in some distant future. An instructional plan should contain several measures of criterion performance even though only one or two are ultimately used.

This chapter has presented two schemes for categorizing multiple criterion measures. It should be noted that other schemes have been proposed. One particularly helpful approach is outlined in Appendix D. The examples provided will assist you by suggesting usable criterion measures as you develop your own objectives and measures.

OBJECTIVES

This chapter has provided instructions so that you might learn to accomplish the following tasks:

1. Identify those measurement procedures which are suitable as criterion measures (i.e., those which measure the behavior called for in the objective).

2. Distinguish between product and process criterion measures.

3. Distinguish between reactive and nonreactive criterion measures.

4. Distinguish between an overall objective, a criterion measure for that objective, and a minimum performance standard to indicate satisfactory attainment of the objective.

5. Derive a number of criterion measures meeting the above standards for an objective.

Complete this practice exercise so that an assessment can be made as to the extent to which this material has been successful. The minimum performance standard for this chapter predicts that 85% of you will be able to attain a perfect score. If the standard set for your performance is not met, the chapter will be modified.

CRITERION TEST

1. Select the alternative most appropriate as a criterion measure for the objective: Learner will decide if a given author is for or against a given political viewpoint.

   Alternative A: Learner will read the author's political essay.

   Alternative B: Learner will describe in writing the author's position and note whether or not the author is favorable to a political action.

   Alternative C: Learner will tell why the author takes a certain political stand.

2. Adjacent to each criterion measure below, indicate which are product and process measures.

   a. safe handling of a power saw

   b. a typed interoffice memo

   c. choral reading in unison

   d. a soldered wire

   e. a set of completed equations

   f. a historical time line

   g. posture while writing

3. For each of the following situations, select the criterion measure which is least reactive:

   Situation: Instructor wishes to determine how many of his students enjoy solving problems in mathematics.

   a. He counts the number of students who raise their hands in response to the question "How many of you enjoyed solving these problems today?"

   b. He collects and tallies responses to a questionnaire which asks if students enjoy solving math problems.

c. He provides a list of free-choice activities and notes how many students elect to solve the math problems listed.

Situation: Instructor wishes to find out if students think it important to keep their workshop machinery in good condition.

a. He counts those who mention this in their list of "Things to do to improve our classroom workshop."

b. He counts those who nod their heads in agreement when he suggests that they keep their workshop machinery in good condition.

c. He observes and counts those learners who volunteer to clean up the workshop and repair the machinery.

4. Label each of the statements below as being either an overall objective (O), the criterion measure (CM), or the minimum level of acceptable performance (MLP).

a. Three-fourths of the learners will correctly sequence all of the steps needed.

b. Learners will be able to correctly sequence the steps necessary to diagnose malfunction in a TV set.

c. Given a scrambled list, learners will unscramble the list and be scored "credit" if all steps are in correct sequence.

ANSWERS TO CRITERION TEST

Your answers to the criterion exercise should have been:

1. B

2. a. Process
   b. Product
   c. Process
   d. Product
   e. Product
   f. Product
   g. Process

3. c.
   c.

4. a. MLP
   b. O
   c. CM

DEVELOPMENT PROCEDURES

It is suggested that you now prepare a test which will enable you to measure the attainment of the objectives selected for your self-instructional package. As you design your test items and scoring procedures, be certain to include some affective measures which would determine if there is a positive attitude toward the package itself.

REVISION DATA SHEET — CHAPTER TWO

PLEASE COMPLETE THIS SHEET AND MAIL TO:

WESTINGHOUSE LEARNING PRESS
2680 HANOVER STREET
PALO ALTO, CALIFORNIA 94304

INSTRUCTIONS: Please mark those answers which you "missed" and comment on your reasoning, sources of confusion, etc.

Practice Exercises: **Criterion Test:**

Page   Page

31. _____ A,B,C   39. _____ 1.A,B,C

32. _____ A,B,C   39. _____ 2.a.
                                                      _____ b.
33. _____ Prod. Meas.   _____ c.
                                                      _____ d.
34. _____ 1.   _____ e.
    _____ 2.   top of page   _____ f.
    _____ 3.   _____ g.
    _____ 4.

34. _____ 1.   39. _____ 3.a,b
    _____ 2.   40. _____ c
    _____ 3.   bottom of page
    _____ 4.   40. _____ a,b,c
    _____ 5.   _____ 4.a.
                                                      _____ b.
36. _____   top of page   _____ c.

36. _____ 1.   bottom half
    _____ 2.   of page

37. _____ 1.
    _____ 2.
    _____ 3.

_____

Name   Teaching Area   School   Date

CHAPTER THREE

Arranging Instructional Activities

Rita B. Johnson

You have already selected your instructional objectives and developed multiple criterion measures for a target group of learners. To arrange an instructional sequence, you must now specify in detail what is needed to accomplish these objectives.

Such a set of specifications is typically produced by advanced planning engineers and then passed on to others who are responsible for the technical production efforts. Instructors, however, usually prepare their own comprehensive lesson plans or sequential units prior to instruction. Once such a unit has been carefully outlined, any instructor should be able to teach from its specifications with minimum difficulty.

Therefore, the purpose of this chapter is to help you in the preparation of an organized self-instructional sequence which will later be produced and tested. This chapter should help you to do the following:

1. Recognize a variety of instructional variables which, when applied, can alter or determine your instructional sequence.

2. Organize an instructional unit which incorporates all aspects of the instructional design thus far, including specifications of what is needed by the instructor and the learner before instruction can occur.

3. Arrange instructional activities and material into a sequential pattern which utilizes a broad variety of instructional variables.

COMMON INSTRUCTIONAL VARIABLES

Below are some of the more commonly accepted variables which research findings suggest affect learning. It may be that not all or any of these are necessary for effective teaching. The instructor must select from as wide a range of alternatives as possible to assure that these variables will be effective. Once he includes them in his instructional sequence, he is in a better position to test empirically whether these variables indeed make a difference.

1. ADVANCE ORGANIZER. An advance organizer is analogous to a preface in a text. It is a statement by the instructor which provides the learner with a cognitive structure or *set*, such as a key phrase which signals the important topic to come.

An example is a paraphrased objective, such as, "Today we are going to learn about the ways in which . . . ," "Our immediate problem is . . . ," and "Let's find out if . . . ."

2. PERCEIVED PURPOSE. A perceived purpose is a question or statement by the instructor which helps the learner to perceive the importance of the instruction to follow. Emphasis here is on the need for the student to perceive that what he is about to do is important or meaningful.

For example, the instructor may ask, "How will solving this problem help us when we try to . . .?" or "How can this be useful to you on the job?" He might also note, "This will make you more efficient when you try to . . . ."

3. ELICITORS. Elicitors are a series of questions or statements designed to produce intended learner responses at successively higher task levels (see Appendix C). Such statements direct the learner to perform in ways which gradually lead to the response specified in the objective. For example:

Recall	Do you recall that objectives are statements of intended behavior changes in the learner?
Comprehension	Stated differently, does this mean that teaching consists of changing the learner's behavior?
Application	What, then, do teachers change when they hope to affect a student's attitude in the classroom?
Analysis	In the film you are about to see, how many attitudinal behavior changes can you identify?
Synthesis	Now write an instructional plan which includes at least three attitudinal changes in your objectives.

Elicitors should be designed to produce a desired or intended response. If the objective calls for discriminating fact from fiction, an elicitor which asks a student to listen to some material may or may not be very helpful, depending upon whether the listening behavior is part of a series which will lead to *discriminating* behavior.

Advance organizers, statements of purpose, and elicitors are motivational in intent. For the objective below, label each numbered item as an *organizer*, a statement of *purpose*, or an *elicitor*. Write *O, P,* or *E.*

Objective: Learner will calculate prices of items which are to be discounted.

1. How will learning to do this help you as a consumer?
2. What is the price of this washing machine, which is to be discounted by one-third?
3. Now let us look at the problem of determining discount prices at a market.
4. Calculate the prices of the following four items.

Answers:

1. Purpose, because it forces the learner to analyze why the learning will be important to him
2. Elicitor, because it elicits the intended behavioral response
3. Organizer, because it organizes or provides a *set* in advance of instruction
4. Elicitor, because it elicits an intended response

4. PROMPT OR CUE. Prompts and cues are hints or aids the instructor provides to help the learner accomplish a desired response. These may be provided when the learner has difficulty or when the instructor wants to ensure success, such as, "Watch out now, I may try to fool you" and "Pay close attention; this problem is complex."

Other common examples of cues are:

Remember, yesterday we said that . . . .

If *this* is true, what about . . .?

When you hear the poem, *listen* for . . . .

As you watch, *notice* whether or not . . . .

Can you find *three* instances where . . . ?

5. PRACTICE. Practice gives the learner opportunity to engage in a specific behavior to be mastered by the end of instruction. Without opportunity to practice relevant or appropriate behavior, the learner is not so likely to perform well on the criterion test.

As in the case of elicitors, there are many opportunities to practice, successively approximating the response specified in the objective. Practice, then, should be consistent with the objective and the criterion measures. Generally speaking, the relationship is as follows:

Objective: A statement is made that a student is expected to perform in a certain way.

Practice: Student is given several chances to perform in that way.

Criterion
Measure: Student is tested on whether he can perform in that way.

For the following objective, which two learning activities are the best examples of relevant practice?

Objective: Learner will label common insects with their scientific names.

1. Reading about the names given to common insects
2. Watching a film on insects
3. Writing the names of insects under pictures of insects
4. Matching pictures of insects with printed names on cards

Answers: 3 and 4

6. SMALL STEPS. Programmers are the foremost advocates of the need for small steps to accomplish learning. How small

each step should be depends in part upon the complexity of the task, difficulty of the content, ability of the learner, and so forth. If the steps are too small, boredom may occur. However, lengthy chunks of content can be tedious and difficult.

7. PACING. Related to the problem of making the learning task simple yet challenging is the problem of whether the sequence moves too fast or too slow. Pacing refers to the rate at which the learner must go through the instructional material or activities.

8. GRADUATED SEQUENCE. Learner behavior can be arranged in successive steps until the criterion performance is reached. Likewise, the activities and content of instruction can be graduated in sequence until they approximate the behavior and content implied in the objective.

A number of logical sequences have been suggested. None, however, has proved significantly better than any other. In fact, some studies have demonstrated that when frames in a programmed sequence are scrambled, learning does *not* significantly decrease.

Commonly used sequences are:

1. simple to complex
2. facts to generalizations
3. concrete to abstract
4. practical to theoretical
5. meaningful to unknown
6. past to present
7. present to future

9. KNOWLEDGE OF RESULTS. Knowledge of results is a response given to the learner which tells him how well he has performed. When a student gets feedback on when and why he is right or wrong, he can take steps to improve and is more likely to give the correct response next time.

Some instructors tell a learner why he is incorrect, then give him an opportunity to try again. In this way, a learner gets additional practice until he makes the appropriate response and can be told he is correct.

10. POSITIVE REINFORCEMENT. A positive reinforcement is anything the instructor does which tends to increase the probability that the student will perform in the same way and repeat his response in the future. Certain instructor behaviors serve as rewards or *reinforcers* for the learner. Such reinforcers are likely to produce similar responses next time.

For example, an instructor's smile, nod of the head, or softening of the voice can reinforce some students. Knowledge of having performed correctly is also a reinforcer.

However, what is reinforcing to one learner may not be to another. It is therefore important to examine the type of reinforcer used and determine its appropriateness for a learner's particular age, sex, and background.

Thus far you have examined a broad variety of instructional variables which can be incorporated into your instructional sequence. Before these can be arranged, however, it will be helpful to detail all other aspects of your instructional system.

PREPARING THE UNIT OF INSTRUCTION

There are many formats which can be used to detail specifications for a unit. A simple one can be found in Appendix E. You should refer to this form now, before you read an explanation of each of the categories listed below.

After filling in the details at the top of the form (if they apply to you) complete the following:

1. PREREQUISITES. List those skills, concepts, and attitudes which you assume the learner possesses upon entering the instructional environment.

2. OBJECTIVES. List the objectives you intend to accomplish as a result of your instructional environment.

3. CRITERION MEASURES. For each objective, list the criterion measures which will enable you to assign scores to observations of student behavior.

4. LEARNER ACTIVITIES. For each objective, list the activities you intend to provide the learner so he may learn to perform intended responses. At this stage, they need not be in any particular sequence. Since this is only a worksheet or mock-up of specifications, brainstorming appropriate activities may be useful. The criterion for selecting such activities is whether they will help the learner to acquire practice needed for accomplishing the objective.

5. RELATED CONTENT. For any activity, there may be reading material which will help the learner respond in appropriate ways. List the exact names, chapters, and pages of relevant books, magazines, or articles which have reference material for use by you or your students during the activity.

6. MEDIA AND MATERIALS. Later you will select and produce a variety of instructional media and materials. At this point, you may want to list audio-visual aids or other media which you suspect are meaningfully related to the activity or the content of the objective. If you know of specific films, filmstrips, slides, photos, recordings, kits, transparencies, or aids, this is a good time to list them.

Again, the criterion for selecting media is whether it will help the learner practice what is needed to accomplish the objective. In this way, the learner is assured of performing well on the criterion test and you are assured of being successful.

Brainstorming may help produce a rich range of alternatives that may prove useful. These can always be discarded later. Remember that if an activity or medium bears no relation to your objective, several alternatives are still possible:

a. A new objective can be added.

b. An existing objective can be modified.

c. The activity or medium can be altered to fit the objective.

d. The activity or medium can be dropped.

Self-checking procedures are needed to confirm your original intentions. Frequently, especially after many changes in your chart, it is wise to check whether all aspects of the chart are internally consistent with your original objectives. A check sheet is provided for this purpose in Appendix F.

Since development of the chart is time consuming, it is suggested you leave the chart and checklist for now and continue studying how to sequence your unit once the chart is completed.

SEQUENCING THE INSTRUCTIONAL ENVIRONMENT

There is more than one way to arrange a unit of work into a sequential pattern. The two suggested here involve:

1. arranging the *content* or lecture material.
2. arranging the learner's *activities* or behavioral responses.

In the first case, the lecture or expository material is simply written out in some logical order (e.g., from simple to complex) and divided into small units at appropriate points. Each small unit then becomes a *frame* to which may be added a variety of instructional variables.

For example, to each frame might be added the following:

1. an advance organizer
2. a statement to provide purpose
3. elicitors
4. prompts to cue the correct response
5. an opportunity to respond (i.e., practice)
6. immediate feedback to the learner on how well he has responded

It is not necessary that these variables be repeated with regularity in each frame. For example, intermittent prompts (i.e., cueing heavily at first, then gradually reducing cues until they are no longer needed) are effective. Withdrawal of prompts allows the learner to approximate the behavior most like the criterion test performance (which will offer him no prompts at all).

At any rate, the inclusion of small steps, prompts, opportunities for appropriate practice, and feedback of results is vital for increasing the effectiveness of your sequence.

A second way to arrange a sequence is to list the activities for each objective in graduated sequence (e.g., from simple to complex, as suggested in Bloom's *Taxonomy*).

Again, each activity becomes a frame or small unit of time within which relevant content and a variety of instructional variables may be incorporated.

For example, one simple procedure could be as follows:

    a. Tell the student what he's to do (prompt or elicit).

    b. Let him do it (provide opportunity for practice).

    c. Tell him if he did it (knowledge of results).

It now remains for you to select and develop appropriate media which may considerably alter this tentative sequence.

The test on the following page asks you to recognize the meaning of some important terms. *If the author is successful, 90% of the readers will attain a score of 80% or better.*

CRITERION TEST

In the space provided, write the letter of the statement that best describes each term:

____ 1. Advance Organizer

a. A statement designed to produce an intended response in the learner

____ 2. Perceived Purpose

b. What the instructor does so that the learner is likely to repeat the response next time

____ 3. Elicitor

c. A hint which aids or helps the learner to be successful in his response

d. A measure by which a score can be assigned to judge a learner response

____ 4. Prompts or Cues

e. Arranging activities and related content into manageable "units" of learning

____ 5. Practice

f. An introductory statement which provides a set for learning

g. Rate at which learners must work through the material

____ 6. Small Steps

h. A statement telling a learner whether or not he is responding correctly

____ 7. Pacing

i. When the learner believes that what he's about to do is important to him

____ 8. Graduated Sequence

j. Arranging a sequence of activities so that they gradually approximate the behavior in the objective

____ 9. Knowledge of Results

k. An activity which provides opportunity to engage in the intended behavior

l. A statement of what learner is to do as a result of instruction

____ 10. Positive Reinforcement

ANSWERS TO CRITERION TEST

Below are the answers to the criterion test. If you did not attain a perfect score, you may want to reread the section COMMON IN-STRUCTIONAL VARIABLES.

1.	f	6.	e
2.	i	7.	g
3.	a	8.	j
4.	c	9.	h
5.	k	10.	b

DEVELOPMENT PROCEDURES

It is suggested that you now do the following:

1. Fill out the form in Appendix E. Let others help you brainstorm ideas.

2. When you complete the form, use the check sheet in Appendix F to check for internal consistency with original objectives.

3. For one objective, write an outline of a script for a sequence of instruction which utilizes small steps, prompts, practice, and knowledge of results. Begin by arranging either the *content* material or learner *activities*.

4. When the script outline is completed, consult two or three peers and determine if you have incorporated in your script:

   a. content presented in small steps

   b. frequent practice activities

   c. immediate feedback to the learner on his performance on practice activities.

Modify your script outline until your peers agree that you have included all three.

REVISION DATA SHEET — CHAPTER THREE

PLEASE COMPLETE THIS SHEET AND MAIL TO:

WESTINGHOUSE LEARNING PRESS
2680 HANOVER STREET
PALO ALTO, CALIFORNIA 94304

INSTRUCTIONS: Please mark those answers which you "missed" and comment on your reasoning, sources of confusion, etc.

Practice Exercises:

Page

49. _____ 1.

_____ 2.

_____ 3.

_____ 4.

50. _____ 3.

_____ 4.

Criterion Test:

Page

56. _____ 1.

_____ 2.

_____ 3.

_____ 4.

_____ 5.

_____ 6.

_____ 7.

_____ 8.

_____ 9.

_____ 10.

_____

Name   Teaching Area   School   Date

CHAPTER FOUR

Selecting and Designing Methods and Materials

Rita B. Johnson

The purpose of this chapter is to provide you with step–by–step procedures for the design of a self–instructional package. It will also provide guidelines for the identification and selection of instructional methods and media.

> The selection of methods and materials should
> be based upon the definition of objectives, cri-
> teria, and content or task analysis.

Unless circumstances force you to do so, you should rigorously avoid any commitment to the methods or media you will use until you have completed analysis of your objectives and criterion measures.

The decision is delayed because no one best method exists for any objective. For example, Appendix G lists a broad range of instructional methods, several of which might be appropriate for any one objective.

To illustrate, write in the space below two objectives from your unit.

1. _____

2. _____

Now turn to Appendix G and select three methods which could help accomplish each objective. Consider only those you do not typically use and write them below.

Objective 1:
a. _____   b. _____   c. _____

Objective 2:
a. _____   b. _____   c. _____

If you found it easy to consider some methods of instruction which were new to you, you have already demonstrated a willingness to keep an open mind in searching for alternative methods and materials.

MATERIALS SEARCH

It is a fairly safe assumption that you will save money and time if you can find commercial or other prepared materials which fit your objectives.

Even if you can't find materials that apply directly, you can often borrow bits and pieces and make alterations.

The first step of a materials search is to develop a set of descriptors for the subject of instruction. The ERIC (Educational Research Information Center) thesaurus is a useful tool to start your descriptor list. These descriptors facilitate your combing through the countless media catalogs much like those descriptors you use in your library research.

A new source that can help in your materials search is *Learning Directory**, a comprehensive guide to instructional media of all kinds using a *subject-keyed* listing that permits quick reference to almost any instructional topic you can think of. Each listing gives detailed descriptors, enabling you to narrow the field quite rapidly.

You have probably had experience obtaining material on preview. Most commercial companies are willing to mail review copies or materials on approval. Rental libraries are a good source of materials.

When you preview materials, you should work from a standardized form to assure uniform judgment. If the material appears promising, take notes, or in the case of a film or video tape, make an audio tape of the soundtrack. This will enable you to integrate the content while you are waiting for the material to be acquired.

There are three possible outcomes of your search: (1) You may find the right material at the right level in the right quantity. (2) You may not find enough or any appropriate materials; thus you will have to develop your own. (3) You may find an overabundance of material; thus you will have to produce further criteria for limiting selection.

The two things to remember in material selection are: (1) Let your objectives guide your material search. Don't start with a film, textbook or some other form of medium you like and then justify its use. (2) Make your search as broad as possible.

Hopefully, you have already selected two or three methods and have located several material packages to accomplish your objectives. The major reason for the selection of these methods and materials should have been that they are most effective for accomplishing the objective.

---

*Learning Directory: 1970-71 (New York: Westinghouse Learning Corporation, 1970).

The final selection must be based on some practical considerations. Besides costs, these are the time allowed to gain the objective, the number of students who will take the unit, the available classrooms, and the instructional machinery.

Can you recall the major reason for selection of methods and materials, as well as three practical considerations?

Major Reason

1. _____

Practical Considerations

1. _____

2. _____

3. _____

ANSWERS:

Major Reason

1. They help you accomplish the objective.

Practical Considerations

1. Cost

2. Time available

3. Student numbers

4. Available classrooms

5. Machinery available

PRINCIPLES OF SELECTION

> *The first principle in medium selection is to consider the instructor as a medium of instruction.*

The instructor is the most expensive medium in an instructional system. At least 60 percent of the operating budget of most school districts goes to certified salaries.

Consider the efficient and professional use of the instructor as a medium of instruction. He is the key factor in the process of individualization. First, he is the most *flexible* of all media. He can change pace, rate, and even content in response to the learner's condition. Second, he is the most *responsive* of all media. He can feel and react uniquely to unique questions. He can build pyramids of associations. He can tie content specifically to an individual learner's interests. He can adjust content to an individual student's ability level. Note that these unique advantages of the instructor are lost when the class size is too large for two–way communication between learner and instructor.

> *The second principle in medium selection is to consider all of the parts which are required to have a self-contained unit.*

Self–contained means the complete set of materials and media which by themselves are necessary and sufficient to achieve an instructional objective. For example, an overhead projector and a set of transparencies are not sufficient. They support a teacher in the presentation of information. The teacher's cost must be included in describing such a unit. On the other hand, a tape and tape recorder, linked to a filmstrip and projector, may be sufficient to achieve an objective and therefore is a self–contained unit.

> *The third principle in determining media is to translate media costs into a cost per student hour for comparison purposes.*

This is a necessary step in convincing budget–minded administrators and trustees of the utility of an instructional approach. Appendix H offers a model for making cost comparisons, assuming that you are faced with a choice between an instructor plus overhead set vs. a tape-filmstrip set.

The cost comparison in Appendix H illustrates principle 1 above. The unit cost of an instructor plus *supporting media* is almost always higher than for a self-contained media package because the instructor is the most expensive element in the system. However, teachers are a superior medium of instruction if they utilize their skills properly.

> *The fourth principle in media selection is to purchase instructional equipment only if you have sufficient material to use the equipment 20 or more hours per week.*

This principle relates to having enough operational hours at your institution to reduce the cost per hour to a low figure. The more you use a piece of equipment, the more efficiently it is being used. This leads to the fifth and final principle.

> *The fifth principle in medium selection is to purchase media in terms of the objectives of major curriculum units.*

To achieve a sufficient base for the justification of equipment, the aims and objectives of more than one class may have to be considered. The medium applications with high initial costs, such as audio-tutorial, dial access, computer-assisted instruction, and most forms of closed-circuit television, can only be justified if they are used in the entire curriculum. But, if used for the entire curriculum, these general medium approaches may be the cheapest.

ORIGINATING MATERIAL

One factor which will influence your development of original materials is availability of production facilities on the campus. In general the smallest educational institution can afford the equipment to produce the following materials:

Visuals — 35 mm slides; 35 mm filmstrips; overhead transparencies; 8 mm motion pictures

Sound — audio tapes

None of the above materials requires expensive facilities. Production can be done by well–trained students or the instructional staff. The production of video tapes requires more expensive equipment and technicians with more skill. But if this medium is used properly, the results are worth the effort.

This chapter will direct your design efforts towards a media system which has proven effective in an educational setting, the *audio-tutorial approach*. This approach should not limit your method selection since it contains all of the medium forms which can be used individually in the classroom. That is, it already includes the use of an instructor in small and large group discussions, yet provides for self-instructional audio-tutorial lessons.

CHARACTERISTICS OF AN AUDIO-TUTORIAL LESSON

An audio-tutorial lesson is an audio tape combined with either a workbook, a filmstrip, a slide or an 8 mm film loop, or some combination thereof. The student takes the lesson to a study carrel where he controls the equipment. The lesson may include an exercise or an experiment. The audio tape controls the entire lesson, and the student is in complete control over all medium sources.

Among the characteristics of the audio-tutorial lesson are:

1. It can integrate several forms of material such as films, slides, and filmstrips.

2. It is self-contained.

3. It may be stored and used repeatedly for many years.

4. It is individualized in that the student can take the lesson at his own convenience, proceed through a series of lessons at his own pace, and modify the sequence and/or content of instruction, depending on his needs and ability.

5. It is only the machine element of a man-machine system. The necessary human portion of the system consists of an instructor interacting with students individually or in small discussion groups. The instructor makes the information meaningful to the student by associating it with his interests and needs and by dealing with his individual learning problems.

The audio-tutorial lesson is under the control of the student. He may proceed at his own pace, repeating parts of the lesson as many times as necessary. He may take the lesson any time the laboratory is open.

The audio–tutorial lesson is especially useful when comparing, analyzing, problem solving, or drilling is required. At the same time, the instructor is free to meet with individuals, small groups, and large assemblies to tutor, clarify, amplify, evaluate, and encourage or inspire.

Now summarize your progress at this point. You are now developing a self–instructional unit which will need to be tested shortly on a few students. You may wish to direct your efforts toward developing a tape-controlled system, such as the audio tutorial. Or, you may wish instead to develop a series of self–instructional activities, none of which will be controlled by audio tape. Neither system will restrict your selection of methods or materials in any fashion. In fact, it should increase the possible alternatives.

PREPARING AN AUDIO-TUTORIAL OR SELF-INSTRUCTIONAL LESSON

Step 1: From your unit of instruction, select a large segment of content or lecture material which is clearly related to one objective and write a *sequential script*. Be certain to utilize a few instructional variables to improve learning (e.g., small steps, perceived purpose, prompts, appropriate practice, knowledge of results).

Step 2: Write down on one-half of a sheet of paper what you say and on the other half what you would write on the chalkboard.

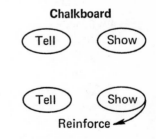

Narration	Chalkboard
"You usually **tell** the students more than you **show** them on the chalkboard."	Tell Show
"You **show** them what you want to **reinforce**."	Tell Show Reinforce

Step 3: Analyze what you have said in the lesson for potential *visualization*.

>   a. First look at your nouns and adjectives. Are you describing something which you could visualize by a picture, a graph,

or an outline? Use visual aids whenever they truly *add* to the effectiveness of your presentation.

b. Examine your verbs and adverbs. Are you describing an action, an activity, or a motion which could be shown rather than explained? This examination for implied motion should be done carefully. For instance, when you describe causality, you are describing motion. When you describe associations on multiple levels, you are describing motion. When you discuss dimensions, you can often explain a fourth dimension by the use of motion. The introduction of motion into a lesson generally has positive influence on the student's receptivity.

Narration	Visual
"You could tape your lecture and photograph what is shown on the chalkboard."	Slide: Instructor writing at chalkboard while speaking into a microphone connected to a tape recorder.

c. Circle all nouns and verbs in your script which can be visualized.

d. Indicate the form and content of the visualization as in the example.

e. Change your narration to reflect and support your visualization.

Step 4: Examine your script for possibilities of student *activity or experimentation*. Remember, in the audio–tutorial lab the student will not be tied to the chair. He will be able to get up to examine displays, operate a piece of machinery, or take some action which will result in discovery and understanding. These activities should be implied in your post–test. The student will generally learn more if he has an opportunity for active practice of what he is to learn.

Narration	Action
"At the sound of the chime, you will stop the tape and	Student will stop the tape. Student will circle nouns

circle the nouns and verbs in your script which can be visualized. When you are through, turn the tape on." (Chime sounds)

and verbs to be visualized. Student will turn the tape on again.

Step 5: Now that you have visualized and activated your script, examine it once again for places where you might utilize instructional variables to increase learning effectiveness. (i.e., Are your learning steps *small* enough? Do you need to add *prompts*? Are students finding out if they respond *correctly*?)

Step 6: Now examine the remaining element, *the sound.* The first consideration is the narration; in person or on tape, you can do it yourself or engage someone with a trained voice.

Another consideration is supplementary sound. Are you referring to an object which has a natural sound that can be heard on the tape? Can you use more than one voice, a guest speaker or a dramatic dialogue? Can excerpts of music or choral reading further your objectives?

Examine your script and indicate in the margin any sound possibilities.

Step 7: After you have reworked your script to reflect appropriate activities, the visuals, and the supplementary sound elements, start assembling materials. Note that your visuals fall into three broad classes:

a. GRAPHIC MATERIAL. (Similar to what you write on the chalkboard.) The preparation of these materials should be done carefully since you are creating a permanent record. Use color whenever possible to reinforce learning points. The use of professional lettering equipment or a graphic artist is desirable but not necessary. A careful freehand will probably be clearer to the students than your normal writing on the chalkboard. These graphic visuals can be photographed into filmstrips.

b. PHOTOGRAPHS OF OBJECTS. Here again it is best to start with slides which will later be copied onto a filmstrip. Using modern camera equipment, you can easily make either slides or filmstrips. You may have had experience in the use of a slide camera for family photographs. If you don't have technical assistance, don't be afraid to do your own photography.

c. MOTION PICTURES. There are two classes of motion-picture visuals. The graphic visuals are animated sequences such as found in cartoons. The technique can be effective in explaining subject matter but is more difficult to use than live action. Live action is easily photographed in 8 mm or Super 8. You may be familiar with the equipment and techniques through your family photographing experience.

Step 8: Assemble your visual materials into a set of slides and/or an 8 mm or Super 8 motion-picture film. Now select a student from your target population. Try to choose a slow learner since he will teach you the most about your writing ability. Talk the student through the lesson, allowing him to ask questions freely. Make a tape of your narration and the questions the student asks for reference during revision. If you have made extensive changes, select another student and repeat the process. *Repeat the process as often as necessary to the point where you do not have to make explanations supplementary to the script.* Your multimedia package is now ready for empirical testing. However, if you are preparing a lesson which is to be audio-tutorial, you must complete the final step.

Step 9: Assemble the final audio-tutorial lesson. Prepare a filmstrip from the augmented slide set and tape narration.

There are two ways to tape the final narration. The professional way is for you to record in a sound booth while observing a student who is listening and working through the lesson. This will give you cues for proper pacing.

The other way is slightly less effective but much simpler. Borrow a good tape recorder, and make the recording in a quiet room. The problem is that you must make a conscious effort to avoid sounding pedantic. It is difficult to keep a natural tone in your voice when speaking to a microphone. Keep in mind that you are talking to an individual student and not a class!

CRITERION TEST

The purpose of this chapter was to help you select and originate a broad-ranged methods/materials system. Write *T* or *F*. *If the author is successful, 90% of the readers will attain a score of 80% or more on these true-false items.*

_____ 1. The audio–tutorial system is the only system that individualizes instruction and integrates a variety of media.

_____ 2. For each type of objective there is probably one best method.

_____ 3. Finding commercial materials which fit existing objectives will save you money and time.

_____ 4. One way to ensure uniform judgment of materials to be selected is to work from a standardized form.

_____ 5. Cost, time, size of class, and available machinery are considered to be practical considerations in selecting media.

_____ 6. An instructor should search for a film he knows and likes even if it does *not* fit his objective.

_____ 7. The cost of the teacher must be included in describing a multi-media unit.

_____ 8. The most flexible and responsive medium of instruction is the instructor.

_____ 9. The student controls the pace of an audio–tutorial lesson.

_____ 10. The complete audio-tutorial system includes use of instructors interacting with students individually or in small and large discussion groups.

ANSWERS TO CRITERION TEST

The answers to this test follow and can be verified by rereading the chapter:

1.	F		6.	F
2.	F		7.	T
3.	T		8.	T
4.	T		9.	T
5.	T		10.	T

DEVELOPMENT PROCEDURES

To complete the preparation of your self–instructional package, you should be ready to do the following:

1. Complete the sequential script (including visualization, activation, and sound) which is designed to accomplish your objectives.

2. Make certain that you have provided for small steps, prompting, practice, and knowledge of results within the script.

3. Prepare the materials with sufficient directions for the learner to work through the package without additional help from you.

4. Prepare to test your system empirically on up to four learners who will be able to help you refine the system before its final implementation with the total learner group. Read the next chapter before making this test.

REVISION DATA SHEET — CHAPTER FOUR

PLEASE COMPLETE THIS SHEET AND MAIL TO:

WESTINGHOUSE LEARNING PRESS
2680 HANOVER STREET
PALO ALTO, CALIFORNIA 94304

INSTRUCTIONS: Please mark those answers which you "missed" and comment on your reasoning, sources of confusion, etc.

Practice Exercises: **Criterion Test:**

Page   Page

65. _____ 1.   73. _____ 1.
    _____ 1.   _____ 2.
    _____ 2.   _____ 3.
    _____ 3.   _____ 4.
                                                      _____ 5.
                                                      _____ 6.
                                                      _____ 7.
                                                      _____ 8.
                                                      _____ 9.
                                                      _____ 10.

| Name | Teaching Area | School | Data |

CHAPTER FIVE

Refining the Instructional System

Rita B. Johnson

This chapter presents a procedure for the empirical testing and revision of an instructional unit, component, product, or program. It deals with the need for successive refinements to the initial draft of a proposed unit of instruction.

Lesson plans, units, courses of study, or any reproducible sequence of instruction designed to produce observable changes in learner behavior must undergo empirical tests and modification. Successive tryouts and revision prior to actual instruction significantly heighten the probability of successful implementation.

The instructor who seeks to attain his objectives will want to test the material on small groups of learners (two to five students) prior to its full-scale implementation. He will examine learner responses carefully and make appropriate modifications in the material to increase the likelihood of learner achievement. He will then test the modified material with a new group of learners and make further refinements until a specified level of performance is achieved by all learners.

This chapter will enable you to:

1. List three categories of problems likely to be found in instructional material during an empirical tryout.

2. Cite examples of specific instructional improvements which can be made in light of learner responses received during an empirical tryout.

3. Describe five procedures for obtaining learner responses during an empirical tryout to eliminate superfluous or confusing characteristics of the instructional material.

COMMON PROBLEM AREAS

In the early stages of developmental testing, an instructor can study the individual learner as he learns. Obtaining feedback from the student, of course, is not new. Even when lecturing, an instructor may ask for questions leading to further examples, restatements, and so forth. This process may lead to a complete revision of the original lecture.

What is relatively new, however, is the notion of closely observing an individual learner at work in the early stages of a program design. Rather than taking lengthy chunks of finished material into the classroom, the instructor should test small parts of his unfinished design with a single learner. Ideally the feedback from learner to instructor begins early, proceeds word by word, element by element, and ceases only when the instructional researcher has achieved his goal — an effective teaching tool.

What is vital here is the notion that the learner is going to teach you. The learner cannot fail, for if he does not achieve what you want him to, your material has failed. Then you must try something else. In fact, in the absence of anything better it might be best to trust your intuition and vary your approach until you are successful. Then edit the material and try it on another learner. Make whatever changes are necessary for your material to take care of both learners. After three or four tries, each with a different learner or group of learners, you will have instruction that is more likely to accomplish its objective than before.

Many writers insist that the first draft should fail to achieve the predicted goal if it is to make full use of data from the learner being tested. If the instruction is a total success on the first trial, the learner has been deprived of an important opportunity to contribute to the design of your instruction. Typically, the first draft will elicit learner responses of 70 percent correct by approximately 70 percent of the tryout learners.

During your trial runs you may find problems which fall into three distinct categories:

1. CLARITY. A need for rewording or rearrangment of material to improve the sentence structure, vocabulary, explanation, instruction, or question

2. ATTENDING. A need to heighten interest to gain attention, arouse curiosity, and provide a challenge to lessen distraction, boredom, or apathy

3. INSTRUCTIONAL VARIABLES. A need to improve the presentation in regard to pace, sequence, organization, size of learning steps, use of prompts, opportunities for practice, or reinforcement

Three categories of problems which are likely to be uncovered while empirically testing your instruction have been cited. What are these three categories? If you wish, reread the three definitions.

1. _____ 2. _____ 3. _____

Below, write what you consider to be an example of a specific revision you might make to solve a problem in each category.

Clarity: _____

_____

Attending: _____

_____

Instructional variables: _____

_____

Examples of ways to improve *clarity* might be to reword the instruction, add a clarifying example, simplify an explanation, change the vocabulary, shorten the sentence, or add a definition.

Problems in *attending* might be lessened by adding humor, eliminating a distraction, providing a sense of purpose, or adding an arousing or attention–getting segment.

Instructional variables may be improved by providing more practice activities, adding cues or prompts, rewarding the learner more frequently, shortening or lengthening the number of steps in an activity, slowing the pace, or reorganizing the sequence of activities.

Below is a list of modifications you might make when you try out and revise your own instructional program. Indicate with letters which ones you believe to be directed toward solving problems of clarity (C), attending (A), and instructional variables (I).

_____ 1. Make instructions clearer.

_____ 2. Attract the student's attention.

_____ 3. Reword the question.

_____ 4. Change the vocabulary.

_____ 5. Shorten the number of steps in the activity.

_____ 6. Simplifv the explanation.

_____ 7. Give a clarifying example.

_____ 8. Speed up the pace.

_____ 9. Add some humor.

_____10. Add some extra prompts.

_____11. Add a practice exercise.

_____12. Provide a sense of purpose and importance to the activity.

_____13. Reward the learner after the activity.

_____14. Rearrange the sequence of activities.

ANSWERS:

1.	C	8.	I
2.	A	9.	A
3.	C	10.	I
4.	C	11.	I
5.	I	12.	A
6.	C	13.	I
7.	C	14.	I

MULTIPLE PROCEDURES FOR OBTAINING LEARNER RESPONSES

Instructional technologists have developed a variety of procedures for obtaining learner responses to each element of instructional material to eliminate superfluous or confusing portions. A combination of these approaches plus others should be employed.

Regardless of which combination is used, the instructor should adopt a tutor-like approach to his learner and employ a tape recorder to record the empirical test. In this way, later distortions due to memory loss or selective perception are likely to be lessened.

During the tryout, at least five methods for obtaining learner responses might be tried:

1. ERROR-RATE APPROACH. The basic concept here is to collect responses to each item, question, or element in the process, and then analyze and modify those items which produce errors or do not result in the desired learner response.

   By locating such errors, the instructor has clues to what modifications of the material are needed. For example, if the student responds with "I cannot answer that question," there may be a need for additional prompts and practice exercises, or the question may be poorly worded.

2. INTERVIEW TECHNIQUE. This technique seeks reactions or comments during or following a lesson. The instructor may not necessarily want to lead the learner and invite opinions on how an element might be revised. Yet, when the learner does make an error, the instructor uses that error and candid comments of the learner to modify the materials.

   For example, when the learner says "I guess I wasn't paying much attention," lack of interest is suspected. The answer may be to include material which will arouse curiosity or challenge the learner.

3. DIAGNOSTIC-CRITERION TEST APPROACH. The diagnostic test, in addition to the regular criterion test, is used to determine the degree of attainment of all prerequisite tasks or behaviors needed prior to accomplishing the criterion test. Diagnostic errors suggest which sections of a program need to be deleted, expanded, or reworked.

   For example, in developing a mathematics program, the instructor may wish to find out which elements of the program need expansion and more thorough treatment. Analysis of the errors on a diagnostic test will tell him which tasks or concepts need to be taught more carefully before the student can be expected to master all the objectives.

4. LATENCY OF RESPONSE APPROACH. Studies indicate that delay in responding to an item is an effective clue for identifying item deficiency. Latency of response (even when the correct response is eventually given) tells the educator when the learner is experiencing difficulty and when parts of the material need to be revised to improve student performance.

For example, if a learner indicates he wants to "think about it for a while," the instructor has a clue as to where a modification of the material is needed. The student may be confused, the material may be ambiguous, or the material may be too difficult.

5. BLACKOUT RATE PROCEDURE. This method eliminates extraneous parts within a lesson by deleting or covering (with paper, black crayon, or ink) all learner activities or expository material deemed nonessential in producing a desired response. In this manner, the instructor has a guide to determine how much might be deleted without increasing errors.

Therefore, if you have a hunch that certain material or activity is superfluous, you might try deleting it to see whether it makes a difference. It has been demonstrated that over 50 percent of existing material may be blacked out without significant increase in errors. This means you may delete half of your instruction and cut your teaching time in half without decreasing learning.

Thus far, five approaches for obtaining learner responses have been discussed. These are: (1) error rate, (2) interview, (3) diagnostic test, (4) latency of response, and (5) blackout. Which procedure do you think is being used in each instance below? Write the number of the procedure next to each example.

_____ a. The learner spontaneously says, "I don't like this."

_____ b. Instructor asks for additional comments about any aspect of the lesson.

_____ c. An instructor of English composition gives a vocabulary test.

_____ d. Several learners respond that they're "thinking it over."

_____ e. The instructor elects to omit the first half of his lesson.

_____ f. Instructor notes that three learners didn't follow a specific instruction.

_____ g. Instructor decides *not* to tell his favorite joke.

_____ h. Learners complain that an assignment was dull.

_____ i. Instructor notes that when she asks a question no learner responds immediately.

_____ j. Of ten learner responses given in a lesson, four are judged inappropriate.

ANSWERS:

a. Interview (2)

b. Interview (2)

c. Diagnostic Test (3)

d. Latency of Response (4)

e. Blackout (5)

f. Error Rate (1)

g. Blackout (5)

h. Interview (2)

i. Latency of Response (4)

j. Error Rate (1)

CONCLUSION

The purpose of this chapter was to provide you with procedures for improving the initial design of instructional material and activities. Empirical testing of your proposed program in the form of several try-out and revision cycles was suggested to help you refine and upgrade the effectiveness of your material.

It is apparent, of course, that such developmental testing can be costly and time consuming. In fact, it would be difficult to empirically try out every lesson, activity, or component prior to its implementation. The saving in learner time on an empirically tested unit of instruction, however, may more than repay the investment of time and energy spent on testing and revising that unit.

The tester must do more than observe, make a tape recording, and take notes. He must be sensitive to overt expressions of thinking by the students. He must notice gaps, predict confusions, sense response failures, rewrite items on the spot, and elicit honest responses. He must let the learner teach him without being defensive. This humility and responsiveness to criticism comes hard to many instructors. Such a person must learn from the mistakes of one learner, capitalize upon them when faced with a new learner, and consistently improve upon the material's effectiveness.

Since only a few learners are being tested at this early stage, they are not a very representative sample of those in the actual instructional setting. Can one really learn much by observing only one learner? Amazingly, one is infinitely better than none! You probably will find that observation of even one learner can significantly improve your first draft of a program. Hopefully, you will have an opportunity to make three or four empirical tryouts and revisions, and each cycle of modification should move you toward your goal of a high level of mastery attained by all learners being tested.

CRITERION TEST

If the author of this chapter has been successful, 90 percent of the readers should now be able to take the following criterion test and attain a perfect score.

1. Below are five procedures for eliminating superfluous or confusing elements in instructional material. Write the letter of the statement that best describes each procedure:

_____ Error Rate   a. Deleting superfluous material to see if needed

_____ Diagnostic–Criterion Test   b. Determining length of time for learner to respond

_____ Latency of Response   c. Obtaining spontaneous, candid comments from learner

_____ Interview Approach

d. Determining most frequent mistakes

_____ Blackout Approach

e. Determining if student has mastery over certain skills

2. Three general categories of problems are likely to be uncovered during an empirical tryout of instructional material. Give two examples of each.

a. Clarity: _____

_____

b. Attending: _____

_____

c. Instructional variables: _____

_____

3. List six examples of material revisions which might be made in your instructional material after an empirical test.

a. _____

b. _____

c. _____

d. _____

e. _____

f. _____

ANSWERS TO CRITERION TEST

1. Error Rate: d
   Diagnostic–Criterion Test: e
   Latency of Response: b
   Interview Approach: c
   Blackout Approach: a

2. (See Page 80.)

3. (See Pages 81 and 82.)

DEVELOPMENT PROCEDURES

To carry out an empirical test of your completed self-instructional package, you can now perform the following steps:

1. Try out your program on from one to four learners. In light of learner response, make necessary modifications in your draft.

2. Try out the revised program on another small set of learners and make necessary revisions.

3. Try out your refined program on a third set of learners and refine once again.

Finally, it will be worth your time to go back and examine the combination of *methods* you used and the *problems* that emerged during each empirical test. Did you try to improve clarity, attending, or instruction variables? What revisions did you make? Are you moving toward your original system goal of a specific level of learner mastery over the instructional material?

REVISION DATA SHEET — CHAPTER FIVE

PLEASE COMPLETE THIS SHEET AND MAIL TO:

WESTINGHOUSE LEARNING PRESS
2680 HANOVER STREET
PALO ALTO, CALIFORNIA 94304

INSTRUCTIONS: Please mark those answers which you "missed" and comment on your reasoning, sources of confusion, etc.

Practice Exercises: **Criterion Test:**

Page   Page

80. _____ Clarity   _____ 12.   86. _____ ER
    _____ Att.   _____ 13.
    _____ I-V   _____ 14.   _____ DCT
81. _____ 1.   84. _____ a.   _____ LR
    _____ 2.   _____ b.
    _____ 3.   85. _____ c.   87. _____ IA
82. _____ 4.   _____ d.   _____ BOA
    _____ 5.   _____ e.   87. _____ Clarity
    _____ 6.   _____ f.
    _____ 7.   _____ g.   87. _____ Att.
    _____ 8.   _____ h.   87. _____ I-V
    _____ 9.   _____ i.
    _____ 10.   _____ j.   87. _____ No. of examples
    _____ 11.   missed

Name   Teaching Area   School   Date

APPENDICES

THE CLASSIFICATION OF EDUCATIONAL OBJECTIVES
Psychomotor Domain*

1.0 *Perception* – the essential first step; the process of becoming aware of objects, qualities, or relations by way of sense organs

    1.1 *Sensor stimulation* – the impingement of a stimulus upon one or more of the sense organs

        1.1.1 Auditory

        1.1.2 Visual

        1.1.3 Tactile

        1.1.4 Olfactory

        1.1.5 Kinesthetic

    1.2 *Cue selection* – identification of the cue or cues and associating them with the task to be performed

    1.3 *Translation* – relating of perception to action in performing a motor act: the mental process of determining the meaning of the cues received for action

2.0 *Set* – a preparatory adjustment or readiness for a particular kind of action or experience

    2.1 *Mental set* – readiness in the sense of having made the anatomical adjustments necessary for a motor act to be performed

    2.2 *Emotional set* – readiness in terms of attitudes favorable to the motor acts. Willingness to respond is implied.

---

*Adapted from Elizabeth Jane Simpson, "The Classification of Educational Objectives, Psychomotor Domain" (Project Report, University of Illinois, 1966).

3.0 *Guided response* – an early step in the development of skill. Emphasis is upon the abilities which are components of the more complex skill.

    3.1 *Imitation* – the execution of an act as a direct response to the perception of another person performing the act

    3.2 *Trial and error* – trying various responses, usually with some rationale for each response, until an appropriate response is achieved

4.0 *Mechanism* – the habituation of a learned response. At this level, the learner has achieved a certain confidence and degree of skill in performance of the act.

5.0 *Complex overt response* – the individual can perform a motor act that is considered complex because of the movement pattern required; a high degree of skill has been attained; the act can be carried out smoothly and efficiently.

    5.1 *Resolution of uncertainty* – the act is performed without hesitation; the individual knows the sequence required and so proceeds with confidence.

    5.2 *Automatic performance* – the individual can perform a finely coordinated skill with a great deal of ease and muscle control.

TAXONOMY OF EDUCATIONAL OBJECTIVES
Affective Domain*

1.0 *Receiving* – attending

    1.1 *Awareness* – conscious of a situation, object, state of affairs

    1.2 *Willingness to receive* – giving attention but neutral toward the stimulus

    1.3 *Controlled or selected attention* – selection of stimuli to be attended to: attention controlled by the learner

2.0 *Responding*

    2.1 *Acquiescence in responding* – compliance or obedience

    2.2 *Willingness to respond* – voluntary response: proceeding from one's own choice

    2.3 *Satisfaction in response* – behavior accompanied by a feeling of pleasure, zest, or enjoyment

3.0 *Valuing*

    3.1 *Acceptance of a value* – shown by consistency of response to the class of phenomena with which a belief or an attitude is identified

    3.2 *Preference for a value* – sufficient commitment to a value so the individual will pursue, seek out, or want it

    3.3 *Commitment* – belief involves a high degree of certainty bordering on faith; includes loyalty to a position, group, or cause; shown by efforts to convince others

---

*Adapted from David R. Krathwohl et al., *Taxonomy of Educational Objectives, Handbook II: Affective Domain* (New York: McKay, 1964).

4.0 *Organization*

    4.1 *Conceptualization of a value* – shown by attempts to identify characteristics of an object or position valued and by expression of judgments about a value

    4.2 *Organization of a value system* – bringing together a complex of values into an ordered relationship

5.0 *Characterization by a value or value complex*

    5.1 *Generalized set* – the individual acts consistently in accordance with the values he has internalized

    5.2 *Characterization* – having developed a consistent philosophy of life or a code of behavior which becomes characteristic of the individual

TAXONOMY OF EDUCATIONAL OBJECTIVES
Cognitive Domain*

1.0 *Knowledge* — Recall of specifics, pattern, structure, etc.

    1.1 Knowledge of specifics — specific bits of information

        1.1.1 Knowledge of terminology

    1.2 Knowledge of ways and means of dealing with specifics — organizing

        1.2.1 Knowledge of conventions — usages, styles, practices, forms

        1.2.2 Knowledge of trends and sequences — with respect to time

        1.2.3 Knowledge of classification and categories — arrangements, classes

        1.2.4 Knowledge of criteria — judging facts, principles, opinion, criteria

        1.2.5 Knowledge of methodology — techniques, methods of inquiry

    1.3 Knowledge of universals and abstractions — theories and generalizations

        1.3.1 Knowledge of principles and generalizations — particular abstractions

        1.3.2 Knowledge of theories and structures — body of principles, range of specific systematic view

Intellectual Abilities and Skills

2.0 *Comprehension* — relating knowledge to other material or seeing the full implication

---

*Adapted from Benjamin S. Bloom et al., *Taxonomy of Educational Objectives, Handbook I: Cognitive Domain* (New York: McKay 1956).

2.1 Translation – paraphrasing or restructuring ideas

2.2 Interpretation – summarization, reorganization

2.3 Extrapolation – extension of trends beyond given data

3.0 *Application* – use of abstractions in concrete situations

4.0 *Analysis* – the breaking down of information into its elements

4.1 Analysis of elements – distinguishing facts from hypothesis, etc.

4.2 Analysis of relationships – connections and interactions of parts of a structure of knowledge

4.3 Analysis of organizational principles – organizational systematic arrangement

5.0 *Synthesis* – putting together of elements and parts to form structure

5.1 Production of a unique communication – communicating to others

5.2 Production of a plan or proposed set of operations

5.3 Derivation of a set of abstract relations – formulating hypotheses or propositions

6.0 *Evaluation* – quantitative and qualitative judgments, using standards of appraisal

6.1 Judgment in terms of internal evidence – logical accuracy, internal consistency, etc.

6.2 Judgment in terms of external criteria – evaluation of internal data in relation to outside influences and selected criteria

CRITERION MEASURES TO DETERMINE LEARNER ACHIEVEMENT*

STANDARDIZED CRITERION MEASURES

1. *Standardized achievement and ability tests,* the scores from which inferences are made regarding the extent to which cognitive objectives have been attained.

2. *Standardized rating scales and check lists* for judging the quality of products in visual arts, crafts, shop activities, creative writing, exhibits for competitive events, cooking, typing, letter writing, fashion design, and other activities.

3. *Standardized tests of psychomotor skills* and physical fitness.

4. *Standardized self-inventories* designed to yield measures of adjustment, appreciations, attitudes, interests, and temperament from which inferences can be formulated concerning the possession of psychological traits (such as defensiveness, rigidity, aggressiveness, cooperativeness, hostility, and anxiety).

TEACHER-MADE CRITERION MEASURES

5. *Achievement tests – objective and essay:* the scores which allow inferences regarding the extent to which specific instructional objectives have been attained.

6. *Rating scales and check lists:* for observation of classroom behaviors; performance levels of speech, music, and art; manifestation of creative endeavors, personal and social adjustment, physical well-being.

7. *Questionnaires:* frequencies of responses to items in an objective format and numbers of responses to categorized dimensions developed from the current analysis of responses to open-ended questions.

---

*Adapted from *A Paradigm Involving Multiple Criterion Measures for the Evaluation of the Effectiveness of School Programs,* by Newton S. Metfessel (University of Southern California) and William B. Michael (University of California, Santa Barbara).

8. *Interviews:* frequencies and measurable levels of responses to formal and informal questions raised in a face-to-face interaction.

9. *Self-evaluation measures:* student's own reports on his perceived or desired level of achievement, on his perception of his personal and social adjustment, and on his future academic and vocational plans.

10. *Peer nominations:* frequencies of selection or of assignment to leadership roles for which the sociogram technique may be particularly suitable.

11. *Projective devices:* casting characters in a class play, role playing, and picture interpretation based on an informal scoring model that usually involves the determination of frequencies of specific behaviors, or ratings of their intensity or quality.

MISCELLANEOUS CRITERION MEASURES

12. *Absences:* full-day, half-day, part-day, and other selective indices pertaining to frequency and duration of lack of attendance.

13. *Anecdotal records:* critical incidents noted including frequencies of behaviors judged to be highly undesirable or highly deserving of commendation.

14. *Attendance:* frequency and duration when attendance is required or considered optional (as in club meeting, special events, or off-campus activities).

15. *Books:* number checked out of library, number renewed, number reported read when reading is required or voluntary.

16. *Changes in program or in teacher as requested by student:* frequency of occurrence.

17. *Choices expressed or carried out:* vocational, avocational, and educational (especially in relation to their judged appropriateness to known physical, intellectual, emotional, social, and aesthetic interests and other factors).

18. *Dropouts:* numbers of students leaving school before completion of program of studies.

19. *Grouping:* frequency and/or duration of moves from one instructional group to another within a given class grade.

20. *Library card:* possessed or not possesed, renewed or not renewed.

21. *Peer group participation:* frequency and duration of activity in what are judged to be socially acceptable and socially undesirable behaviors.

22. *Skills:* demonstration of new or increased competencies such as those found in physical education, crafts, homemaking, and the arts that are not measured in a highly valid fashion by available tests and scales.

23. *Tape recordings and video tapes:* record of critical incidents and of other events that can be analyzed and are amenable to classification and enumeration.

FORMAT REQUIREMENTS

Topic or
Unit:_____

Target
Learners: _____

Block
of Time: _____

Institution: _____

Title of
Course: _____

Instructor's
Name: _____

Prerequisites	Objectives	Criterion Measures	Learner Activities	Related Content	Media and Materials
1.	1.	1. a. b. c. d.	1. a. b. c. d.	1. a. b. c. d.	1. a. b. c. d.
2.	2.	2. a. b. c. d.	2. a. b. c. d.	2. a. b. c. d.	2. a. b. c. d.
3.	3.	3.	3.	3.	3.
4.	4.	4.	4.	4.	4.

FORMAT CHECKLIST

CHECKLIST:

1. Do the students still possess the prerequisites needed as entering behaviors?

2. Are your criterion measures still measuring behavior implied in the objective?

3. Are all learner activities still relevant or helpful in accomplishing the objective?

4. Is all content still related or of help in accomplishing the objective?

5. Are the media and materials still related clearly to some objective? Will their use help students perform well on the criterion test?

METHODS OF INSTRUCTION

The principal methods by which instruction is provided:

Comparative Analysis — A thought process, structured by the teacher, employing the description, classification, and analysis of more than one system, group, or the like so as to ascertain and evaluate similarities and differences.

Conference — A one-to-one interaction between teacher and learner where the individual's needs and problems can be dealt with. Diagnosis, evaluation, and prescription may all be involved.

Demonstration — An activity in which the teacher or another person uses examples, experiments, and/or other actual performance to illustrate a principle or show others how to do something.

Diagnosis — The continuous determination of the nature of learning difficulties and deficiencies, used in teaching as a basis for the selection — day by day or moment by moment — of appropriate content and methods of instruction.

Directed Observation — Guided observation provided for the purpose of improving the study, understanding, and evaluation of that which is observed.

Discussion — An activity in which pupils, under teacher and/or pupil direction, exchange points of view concerning a topic, question, or problem to arrive at a decision or conclusion.

Drill — An orderly, repetitive learning activity intended to help develop or fix a specific skill or aspect of knowledge.

Experimentation — An activity involving a planned procedure accompanied by control of conditions and/or controlled variation of conditions together with observation of results for the purpose of discovering relationships and evaluating the reasonableness of a specific hypothesis.

Field Experience — Educational work experience, sometimes fully paid, acquired by pupils in a practical service situation.

Field Trip — An educational trip to places where pupils can study the content of instruction directly in its functional setting, e.g., factory, newspaper office, or fire department.

Group Work — A process in which members of the class, working cooperatively rather than individually, formulate and work toward common objectives under the guidance of one or more leaders.

Laboratory Experience — Learning activities carried on by pupils in a laboratory designed for individual or group study of a particular subject-matter area, involving the practical application of theory through observation, experimentation, and research, or, in the case of foreign language instruction, involving learning through demonstration, drill, and practice. This applies also to the study of art and music, although such activity in this instance may be referred to as a studio experience.

Lecture — An activity in which the teacher gives an oral presentation of facts or principles, the class frequently being responsible for note-taking. This activity usually involves little or no pupil participation by questioning or discussion.

Manipulative and Tactile Activity — Activity by which pupils utilize the movement of various muscles and the sense of touch to develop manipulative and/or perceptual skills.

Modeling and Imitation — An activity frequently used for instruction in speech, in which the pupils listen to and observe a model as a basis upon which to practice and improve their performance.

Problem-Solving — A thought process structured by the teacher and employed by the pupils for clearly defining a problem, forming hypothetical solutions, and possibly testing the hypothesis.

Programmed Instruction — Instruction utilizing a workbook or mechanical and/or electronic device which has been "programmed" to help pupils attain a specified level of performance by (a) providing instruction in small steps, (b) asking one or more questions about each step in the instruction and providing instant knowledge of whether each answer is right or wrong, and (c) enabling pupils to progress at their own pace.

Project — A significant, practical unit of activity having educational value, aimed at one or more definite goals of understanding and involving the investigation and solution of problems.

Reading — Gathering information from books, periodicals, encyclopedias, and other printed sources of information, including oral reading and silent reading by individuals.

Recitation — Activities devoted to reporting to a class or other group about information acquired through individual study or group work.

Role-Play — An activity in which students and/or teacher take on the behavior of a hypothetical or real personality in order to solve a problem and gain insight into a situation.

Seminar — An activity in which a group of pupils, engaged in research or advanced study, meets under the general direction of one or more staff members for a discussion of problems of mutual interest.

Sensitivity Training — An activity in which a group and a trainer meet to self-consciously examine their immediate feelings and perceptions about themselves and each other in order to gain skill in authentic communication, leadership, behavioral flexibility, or social sensitivity.

Shopwork — An activity emphasizing skill development through experience in woodwork, metal work, or other industrial processes and procedures.

Skill Practice Session — All activity in which pupils have opportunity to put into practice those skills and understandings previously learned through other instructional activities.

PART 1

MODEL FOR MEDIA SET COST COMPARISON

	Instructor Overhead	Tape Filmstrip
1. Equipment Costs		
1. Initial cost of equipment	$150.00	$300.00
2. Amortized for 6,000 hrs of operation (30 hrs/wk x 40 wks/yr x 5 yrs = 6,000 hrs) per hr	.025	.050
3. Maintenance/hr	.010	.020
2. Material Cost		
a. Visuals — 30 frames @ .30 frame @ 30–frame filmstrip	9.00	1.50
b. Narration cost tape		1.50
c. 20% of lesson is revised each x 5 yrs	9.00	3.00
d. Total cost material for 5 yrs	18.00	6.00
e. Per hour, for 6,000 hrs	.003	.001
Media Costs		
3. Total material and equip. cost per hr	.038	.071
4. Instructor time per hr	6.00	
5. Total cost per hr	6.038	.071
6. Per student hr @ 30 students/hr @ 1 student/hr	.201	.071

(EXPLANATION ON FOLLOWING PAGE)

PART 2

EXPLANATION

1. Compute the cost per hour of the equipment. This requires an estimate of the useful life of the equipment in terms of hours of operation. In this case, the estimate is that all of the equipment we are comparing will last five years or for 6,000 hours of operation. It is also estimated that repairs and maintenance for each piece of equipment would cost 1 cent per unit per hour.

2. Compute the cost of the material. Preparation time is not included since it is assumed that it is the same for both types of material. Other assumptions are that there are 30 visual frames in the lesson, that overhead transparencies cost $.30 per frame, and that a 30–frame filmstrip costs $1.50. The instructor supplies the narration that accompanies the transparencies, but a tape costing $1.50 is required for the tape–filmstrip set.

   For purposes of comparison, the life of the basic material is set at five years. It is also predicted that 20 percent of the set will be revised each year. At the end of five years the material will have undergone a 100-percent revision cycle. This total cost can be divided by the 6,000-hour base period for a per-hour cost.

3. The per–hour costs of the equipment and the material are added.

4. The instructor's time is added to the overhead costs to make it a self–contained set. This cost cannot be amortized since the instructor must be present every time the lesson is given. The tape and filmstrip are a *self–contained* set; the instructor's presence is not required.

5. The total set cost per hour is the total of the equipment, material, and instructional costs per hour.

6. Divide the total number of students who will benefit from the lesson at one time by the total cost per hour for the cost per student hour. Assume that the instructor plus overhead lesson is given to 30 students at a time. The filmstrip tape lesson is given to only one student at a time. Note that the *initial* cost of equipment in a tape-filmstrip set is twice that of the overhead. However, the *actual* unit cost is approximately one-third since the cost of the instructor must be added to the cost of the overhead.

If you found *Developing Individualized Instructional Material* useful, you may want to order:

TOWARD INSTRUCTIONAL ACCOUNTABILITY:
A Practical Guide to Educational Change

John E. Roueche   Barton R. Herrscher
University of Texas at Austin   Mitchell College, Statesville, NC

Toward Instructional Accountability: A Practical Guide to Educational Change is designed to meet current needs for staff development, in preservice or in-service training of teachers, counselors, and administrators, with particular emphasis on community college personnel. The author-editors have chosen carefully from current educational literature twenty-one readings that present incisive information on areas of vital importance in considerations of educational change, especially in the areas of accountability and individualization.

Both cognitive and affective learning objectives are specified. Because of the many different learning situations in which this book may be used, the precise behavior or performance for demonstrating mastery of objectives is largely open-ended. Stress is not so much on the means as on the end: *successful learning.*

Each of the ten units is introduced with a statement of the rationale and a list of objectives, followed by related readings. In this way the reader knows what he is expected to learn and can proceed at his own pace.

Unit Titles: A Rationale for Educational Change
              Accountability-Based Instruction
              Individualized Instruction
              Changing Approaches to Teaching
              Specifying the Purposes of Education
              Student Learning: An Emerging View
              Learning for Mastery
              The Assessment of Student Learning
              Evaluating Instructional Programs
              Accountability

ORDER FORM

TOWARD INSTRUCTIONAL ACCOUNTABILITY:
A Practical Guide to Educational Change

Please send me _____ copies of *Toward Instructional Account-ability: A Practical Guide to Educational Change.*

Price: $6.50

NOTE: SINGLE-COPY ORDERS MUST BE PREPAID.
      (Orders for 10 or more copies are discounted 20%.)

☐ Enclosed is my ☐ check ☐ money order.
☐ Please bill me, plus postage.

MAIL TO:
    Westinghouse Learning Press
    P.O. Box 10680
    Palo Alto, California 94303

name	position
school	phone number
address	
city	state zip

ORDER FORM

DEVELOPING INDIVIDUALIZED INSTRUCTIONAL MATERIAL
(a self-instructional material in itself)

Please send me _____ copies of *Developing Individualized Instructional Material* and the Institutional Support Manual, which is included at no extra cost.

Price: $3.75

NOTE: SINGLE-COPY ORDERS MUST BE PREPAID.
        (Orders for 10 or more copies are discounted 20%.)

    ☐ Enclosed is my ☐ check ☐ money order.
    ☐ Please bill me, plus postage.

Mail to:
Westinghouse Learning Press
P.O. Box 10680
Palo Alto, California 94303

name	position
school	phone number
address	
city	state zip